Cultural China

Chinese Customs

闲话中国民俗

Better Link Press

This book is edited and designed by the Editorial Committee of *Cultural China* series

Managing Directors: Wang Youbu, Xu Naiqing
Editorial Director: Wu Ying
Editors: Sam Meekings, Yang Xinci, Yang Xiaohe

Chinese text by Xiang Wei
Translation by Benjamin Chang, Hu Lingque
Photos provided by IC

Interior and Cover Design: Yuan Yinchang, Xia Wei

ISBN: 978-1-60220-104-0

Address any comments about *Chinese Customs* to:

Better Link Press
99 Park Ave
New York, NY 10016
USA
or
Shanghai Press and Publishing Development Company
F 7 Donghu Road, Shanghai, China (200031)
Email: comments_betterlinkpress@hotmail.com

Computer typeset by Yuan Yinchang Design Studio, Shanghai
Printed in China by Shanghai Donnelley Printing Co. Ltd.

1   2   3   4   5   6   7   8   9   10

CONTENTS

CONTENTS

China is an ancient country with a recorded history of over 5,000 years, in the course of which the Chinese people have come up with a large number of inventions and innovations while adapting to the environment around them. Based on careful observation of the course of nature, the Chinese ancestors formulated the lunar calendar. According to the lunar calendar a year is divided into twenty-four seasonal points in order to regulate life and production. This has also given rise to many traditional Chinese festivals, which are particularly important to the Chinese people. People use these holidays to relax from the daily toil and enjoy life to its fullest. For Chinese people, dining is one of the most pleasurable activities. Therefore, a diverse food culture has been developed over hundreds of years.

China is a vast country. Different customs and ways of looking at the world have gradually developed. As the saying goes, habits differ within a radius of ten miles and customs within a hundred miles. If you travel thousands of miles, you will find a huge difference in ways of living. However, there are still a huge number of customs that have become established over the centuries and these customs have become permanent traditions, ingrained in society as an integral part of Chinese culture.

Holidays

The Spring Festival

The Spring Festival, or the Chinese New Year, is by far the most important Chinese holiday, celebrated with the most fanfare and for the longest duration. In 1949, following the founding of the People's Republic, the Gregorian calendar was adopted for use and January 1 was designated as New Year's Day, otherwise known as the Solar New Year's Day. The beginning of a new year according to the traditional Chinese calendar usually comes around the time of *Lichun*, the Beginning of Spring. Hence the name of the Spring Festival, or the Lunar New Year.

To the Chinese the celebration of the Spring Festival means the celebration of the New Year. The first three days of the lunar calendar are a legal holiday in China, set aside for elaborate celebrations, which vary throughout the country depending on local customs, though most involve family reunion dinners, firecrackers, scrolls, and dragon dances. Celebrations last well beyond these three days; they actually begin on the last day of the lunar calendar and continue till the fifteenth day of the first month, which is known as the Lantern Festival.

A family get-together is a must at the Spring Festival.

The last day of the lunar calendar is called Lunar New Year's Eve, and this is when the family reunion dinner takes place. People spend days working in the kitchen to make sure that a sumptuous feast is ready for the occasion. In some big cities, husband and wife are both occupied at work and more often than not choose to dine out.

Some people make an effort to stay up throughout the night. This practice is known as "keeping the old age", and it has a dual purpose: to look upon the past year with nostalgia, and to look forward to a joyful new year. As the countdown reaches zero, deafening fireworks rocket into the starry night, both in cities or in villages, bidding farewell to the old year and ushering in the new. In parts of northern China, tradition dictates that aside from generous portions of pastry, fruits, and melon seeds piled up on the table, a full plate of rice, cooked beforehand, should be

A clay figurine is being made on the spot to accentuate the holiday atmosphere.

presented for sacrificial purposes. It is named "The Meal of the Previous Year", which implies that there are always leftovers or a surplus at the year's end.

On New Year's Day, greetings are exchanged with in-laws and friends. In the past, this ritual took place within the family. First thing in the morning, members of less seniority in a family had to take the initiative to give New Years' blessings to their elders, wishing them good luck and a long life. In return, they received "red envelopes". Nowadays, most young couples live apart from their parents. Therefore, they visit the latter's residences to extend holiday wishes. On this day, people in the streets are seen with beaming smiles, and greet old acquaintances with the ubiquitous "Happy New Year!"

Thanks to modern advances in communication technology, holiday greetings are increasingly extended by telephone, text messaging, and e-mail, superseding the older traditions. Text messaging is nowadays very popular among the younger generation: it is not uncommon for China's telecommunication companies to register sizable profits from well-wishers on the two busiest days of the Spring Festival.

Children look at a lion dancer during the first day of Lunar New Year.

Tradition dictates that on the second and third days following the Spring Festival Day, married daughters should

It is trendy to exchange Chinese New Year's greetings by text messaging.

visit their childhood homes accompanied by their husbands and children. In the countryside, candies, fruits, and other snacks are brought home to be distributed among the neighbors in order to show affection. These two days are also a good occasion for meeting with distant relatives and friends. These types of large-scale visits are rare during the regular days of the year when everybody is busily occupied. Naturally, people take advantage of the Spring Festival to meet for fun and food, to chat and do a lot of catching up.

The Fifth Day is the day for welcoming the God of Fortune. This practice, very popular during the Ming and Qing Dynasties and Republic years, is still prevalent. Legend has it that the Fifth Day is the birthday of the God of Fortune. It is believed that if on the strike of midnight the windows and doors are left wide open, incense is burned, and fireworks are let off to welcome the God of Fortune, one may be blessed with increased wealth in the new year. This is an important day for businessmen, who usually spend it praying devoutly and burning incense at temples.

Companies and businesses set off firecrackers on the fifth of the first lunar month in expectation of thriving business in the coming year.

The Sixth Day, according to folklore, was originally set aside for "saying good riddance to poverty". On this day, the God of Poverty is to be ceremoniously sent away. The God of Poverty is said to be diminutive in stature, weak, pathetic, and fond of thin rice congee and tatters. The way to say good riddance to this God varies from place to place. Symbolic carts and boats may be prepared, along with pancakes and other foods for his consumption. This custom is an interesting reflection of the universal desire to relegate poorer days to the past, and to encourage the arrival of better days laden with abundance and prosperity.

Origins of the Spring Festival

Chinese holidays are closely associated with legends and myths. Due to their long history and the lack of verifiable data, it is difficult to pinpoint the exact origins of the traditional Chinese holidays.

The origin of the Spring Festival can be explained through stories, legendary, mythical, and folk tales. These tales have enriched traditional Chinese culture with their vivid and entertaining images.

Legend One

Back in time immemorial, there lived in the deep mountains a monster called *Nian*. It was a gigantic, fierce-looking creature, with two long horns and glowing eyes. Ferocious by nature, the monster preyed upon birds, animals, and even humans. *Nian* was reputed to be Lord of the Mountain. Tigers and lions were no match for *Nian*. As for goats and monkeys, they would simply collapse at the sound of its frightening growl.

However, the monster did not limit itself to the mountains. Roughly every 365 days it would creep down into towns and villages to feed on human flesh, always between nightfall and daybreak. This night came to be called *Nian*'s night, and various ways were devised to survive *Nian*'s attacks, such as cooking dinner early, hemming in poultry and cattle, shutting windows, and eating the elaborately prepared "Year's End Dinner" behind locked doors. The fear and uncertainty of the night prompted the entire family to gather together at the dinner table for what was thought to be "the last supper", with the likelihood that they would end up being food for *Nian*. After the dinner, nobody dared to retire but instead sat up until dawn came, and with it safety. This practice of keeping vigil, which originated in the period of Southern and Northern Dynasties, evolved into a custom that is still prevalent today.

Legend Two

In ancient China, due to an unpredictable climate and the absence of a workable calendar, the life and work of the general population offered suffered serious disruption. This aroused the King's deep concern. It so happened that a young woodcutter by the name of Wan Nian became fixated with the idea of ending this chaotic situation. One day, as he took a break from chopping wood in the mountain beneath a tall tree, he noticed that the shadow of the tree changed its location as the sun set. He had a sudden brainwave, and soon invented a sun-dial. Later on, observing a mountain spring rolling down the slope, he invented a five-layered "leaking pot" to measure time. After diligently studying the world around him, he finally came to discover that the four seasons rotated in a cycle of 365 days and that the length of the day light also changed in a fix pattern.

Aware of the King's concerns, Wan Nian, armed with his sundial and "leaking pot", soon presented himself at the court. He explained the astronomical phenomena he had observed to the King. The King, impressed with these new ideas, decided to keep him in his court so that he might conduct further research and figure out the laws which would pave the way for the creation of an accurate calendar.

After years of observation and intensive research, Wan Nian eventually came up with an accurate calendar. When the King visited him one day, Wan Nian told him: "A full twelve months have elapsed and one whole

Spring scrolls are posted in celebration of the Chinese New Year.

year is gone. A new cycle will start. Please name a holiday, sire, for its commemoration." The King replied: "Spring is the start of the new year. Why not call it the Spring Festival?" According to legend, that was how the holiday came into being.

There is no lack of legends on the origin of the Spring Festival. The above two are the most often quoted, the first legend being more mythical than real and the second one more plausible. In either case, there was a happy ending.

Traditional Customs of the Spring Festival

Spring is synonymous with things nature and beauty. There is a wide variety of ways of celebrating this holiday, many of which have survived to this day.

Spring Scrolls

Also known as "spring posters on doors", spring scrolls are carefully-written couplets which are posting on walls, hall pillars, and doors, to mark the happy occasion. Twin scrolls posted at the Spring Festival are termed spring scrolls, and usually carry a message of good luck and joy.

Spring scrolls boast a history of 1,000 years, and the custom was well recorded in ancient archives. They are posted mostly on the doors. Doors in traditional Chinese architecture come in pairs, side by side. Therefore, spring scrolls must also come in a pair. For instance,

Peace reigns every day,

Wealth rolls in every year.

The first line is called the "upper" scroll, and the second line the "lower" scroll. Sometimes, there is a horizontal scroll across the top of the door which accentuates the meanings of the two vertical scrolls. For instance:

Great joy is experienced every spring,

True happiness is felt every year.

Painters and calligraphers are writing spring scrolls.

The horizontal scroll is "The land is alive with the advent of spring".

Spring scrolls are far from easy to compose. The calligraphy should be neat and balanced, and the wording should suggest rhythm and harmony. The couplets call for the tricky use of identical word classes, synonyms, and rhyming. The skills needed to compose these couplets cannot be acquired without strict special training, with the result that the average Chinese is incapable of composing a brilliant spring scroll. Such rigorous demands can be traced to poetry composition in ancient China. China is a nation with a long history and a rich cultural heritage. Its men of letters, both present and past, penned numerous immortal spring scrolls which have been compiled into books for use today, saving one the trouble of racking his or her brains to create a well-written scroll.

Spring scrolls, despite their reliance on beautiful calligraphy and poetic prowess, come in different styles: veiled, outspoken, suggestive, or metaphorical. They are appreciated not only for their beauty but also for their subtle connotations.

Spring scrolls can be seen wherever you go during the Spring Festival, in metropolitan or rural areas, at home or in public. The festive atmosphere of this traditional holiday is never complete without these bright, auspicious objects in sight.

Door Gods Pictures

Door Gods are images of deities posted on doors in order to dispel evil spirits and bring peace. Door Gods are repulsive-looking and ferocious, as they are intended to frighten away monsters and ghouls.

There is an interesting story about the custom of posting Door Gods pictures. Legend has it that Emperor Tai Zong of the Tang Dynasty once fell sick and was assailed with monsters' screams in his dreams. He awoke in a state of fright, then tossed about in bed and could not go back to sleep. The next day he confided his dreams to two of his generals, who then offered to guard his bedroom, fully armed, throughout the night. That night turned out to be calm and peaceful, and the Emperor slept like a log. However, unable to bear to see his two devoted generals on guard outside his bedroom night after night, he ordered their images to be painted on the gate of the imperial palace so that their pictures could do the job instead of them. That is how the practice of posting Door Gods pictures to ward off the evil began.

Couplets are posted on the door to ward off the evil spirits.

Firecrackers

Firecrackers are made of dynamite tightly wrapped in multi-layered paper, with a fuse which, when ignited, sets off an explosion with a loud roar. This practice is said to be originated in the Han Dynasty when a segment of bamboo was heated in a fire, causing the air inside to expand until the bamboo blew up with a loud bang. Since the Tang Dynasty, firecrackers have been made of dynamite and paper, to be let off on happy occasions for celebration purposes. The Spring Festival is the time when most firecrackers are set off, in order to drive away evil spirits.

On New Year's Eve, when the clock strikes midnight, the entire country is enveloped in the sound of roaring firecrackers. However, some people prefer to set off fireworks in the early morning of Lunar New Year's Day in order to "burst open the door for good luck to

Children are playing fireworks for fun on Chinese New Year's Eve.

Children are having most fun on Chinese New Year's Day.

pop in." Following deafening roars, shredded red paper is scattered everywhere. Villages and cities literally become "a sea of red". Unfortunately, the mess poses a big problem for the street sweepers who have to clean it up.

There are many different types of firecrackers. There are loud ones as well as "dumb" ones. The silent ones can blast off with a blaze of colors, however, which is as beautiful as a bouquet of flowers. Some firecrackers have elaborate nicknames, such as "Two Dragons Playing with a Silk Ball," "A Peacock Unfolding its Wings," "Bright Purple and Blazing Red," and "Soaring High".

Firecrackers are always associated with celebration and happy occasions. The custom of setting off firecrackers on holidays and at weddings has been around for centuries. While they bring laughter and excitement, they may sometimes lead to fires and accidents, and have been known to scare the sick, the elderly and young children. Therefore, they are banned in some big cities, especially in downtown areas and around historical buildings.

New Year Posters

Part of the New Year's tradition, New Year Posters are a unique type of painting in China, posted in celebration of the New Year. The history of this ancient folk art form can be traced back to the Song Dynasty. New Year Posters share the same role as Spring Scrolls, namely to ward off evil spirits and bad omens. They reflect popular customs and beliefs, and reflect hopes for the future.

Traditional New Year Posters, usually made from wood engraving and watercolor block printing, are marked by straightforward lines, brilliant colors, and a large amount of details. New Year Posters can also take the form of paper cuttings and paper drawings. New Year Posters cover such themes as the celebration of a bumper crop, blooming flowers and chirping birds, spring scenery, and adorable toddlers. The earliest known New Year Poster in existence is a wood engraving poster painted during the Southern Song Dynasty and entitled "Great Beauties of Sui Dynasty", and it depicts four ladies known for their stunning beauty: Wang Zhaojun, Zhao Feiyan, Ban Ji, and Lu Zhu. The most popular and widely circulated New Year Poster is called "Mouse's Wedding", which depicts a personified mouse following human wedding customs.

New Year Posters vividly reflect local characteristics. Despite different styles which vary from region to region, they all share the common features of pleasing coloring and auspicious messages. Places renowned for their New Year Posters include Yangliuqing in Tianjin, Taohuawu in Jiangsu, Yangjiabu in Shandong, Zhuxianzhen in Henan, and Foshan in Guangdong.

In recent years, traditional Chinese New Year Posters are marketed

Chinese New Year celebration supplies are plentiful.

abroad to the delight of other peoples who are captivated by their vibrant exotic flavor. 2006 saw the Soccer World Cup take place in Berlin. About one hundred artists from various countries submitted posters to be adopted for the event. The award went to a traditional Chinese poster entitled "Hercules' Cup" depicting a chubby boy, with hair shaped like a teapot lid, holding a soccer ball on which the large Chinese character for "Happiness" was written.

Lucky Money

A traditional custom during the Spring Festival is to give children and younger relatives red packets filled with money. This money is considered to be a form of blessing, and is therefore known as "lucky money". Senior members of a family give away this money in the hope that by doing so evil spirits can be warded off.

In the past, lucky money took a different form: hundreds of copper coins were threaded together with red strings into the shape of a carp or a dragon to suggest good luck and longevity. As copper currency was gradually discarded, copper

Lucky money in small red packets is popular.

lucky money gave way to money wrapped in red paper. The amount of money is unimportant, because it is the act of giving which brings good luck. The practice remains popular today.

Food Enjoyment

The most important feature of the Spring Festival is having abundant food. The gathering of the whole family for a banquet is the culmination of a year's hard work. All people, whether they are workers, peasants, or office clerks, put money aside to have a spectacular meal. In the past, the Spring Festival was the only time of year in which many people had the opportunity to eat all they could of exciting or expensive foods. However, this is already becoming a thing of the past. With improved standards of living, choice food becomes affordable all year round. Therefore, people no longer display an insatiable craving for food during the Spring Festival. However, it is still important to include certain foods in the Spring

Dumplings and garlic absorbed in sauce at Xiaoyangguan Restaurant, Beijing.

Festival meals, such as dumplings (*jaozi*), and New Year Cake, which not only satisfy the palate, but also symbolize the hope for a better and more abundant new year.

Jaozi

The custom of eating *jaozi* originated with the Han ethnic group in northern China about 1,400 years ago. *Jaozi* on the New Year's menu suggests good fortune and "smooth sailing". They are seen as a way to bid farewell to the old year and usher in the new. Eating *jaozi* is a very popular part of the Spring Festival and has persisted to this day. In northern China, a host will serve steaming *jaozi* to indicate that the guest is strongly valued.

Jaozi are made from kneaded dough which is cut into dices and flattened into thin round wraps which are stuffed with various fillings. Some of the most popular *jaozi* fillings are pork, beef, mutton, and fish, mixed with celery, parsley or leek. However, any combination of meat and vegetables can serve as the filling.

There are also many different cooking methods, as *jaozi* can be steamed, boiled, or deep fried. Custom dictates that the making of *jaozi* must be completed before twelve o'clock on the last day of the twelfth lunar month. The completion of making "*Jaozi* of the Year" marks the transition from the old year to the new.

New Year Cake

The Chinese call New Year Cake *nian gao*, which is a homophone of "better year", meaning that every year will be better than the previous one.

New Year Cakes come in a wide variety of shapes and sizes, and are usually either sweet, salty or plain. These cakes used to be hand-made via a process of soaking, grinding, drip-drying, mixing the different ingredients, and finally steaming. Nowadays however, the New Year Cakes available at supermarkets are mostly machine-made.

Catering to different local tastes, New Year Cakes vary from region to region. In southern China, they are predominantly either sweet or salty. In Hangzhou and Ningpo, New Year Cakes are made of rice and are steamed, fried, or cooked in soup. The sweet cakes are usually made of sticky rice and mixed with such ingredients as lard, sugar, dried laurel and rose petal, and peppermint. The cooking method involves steaming or deep frying. New Year Cakes made in Guangdong are unique, and include such varieties as

Children are busy making New Year's cake.

Laba porridge

turnip cake, taro cake, golden yellow cake, and water chestnut cake, though ground rice remains the main ingredient.

New Year Cakes in northern China are also usually sweet, including such varieties as red date cake and gingko cake. Deep fried brown rice cake is very popular in northern Shanxi and Inner Mongolia, where the cakes are mixed with red bean paste or jujube paste.

The act of making New Year Cakes is surrounded by superstitions. Since the quality of the cake is believed to affect one's fortune in the year to come, it is important to avoid swearing or arguing while the cake is being prepared.

Laba Porridge

The eighth day of the twelfth lunar month, which is usually the coldest month of the year, is commonly referred to as *laba*. After that day, it is not long until the Spring Festival and so preparations for the big celebration soon begin.

The custom of eating *laba* porridge on that particular day started roughly a thousand years ago. On the night of the seventh day of the twelfth lunar month, people begin the long process of making the *laba* porridge which needs to be simmered from midnight until well into the next morning. *Laba* porridge can be sweet or salty and can contain a numbe of supplementary ingredients. Some *laba* porridges boast over twenty ingredients, such as red dates, lotus seeds, walnuts, chestnuts, almonds, pine nuts, longan meat, hazelnuts, grapes, gingko, water chestnuts, dried rose petals, red beans, and peanuts. The more decorative varieties of *laba* porridge may contain nuts chiseled into the shape of an animal.

Students are learning to cook *laba* porridge under the teacher's guidance.

Old customs require that *laba* porridge be presented first to Gods and ancestors for sacrificial purposes before it is shared with friends and relatives (who must receive it before midday). Finally it is the family's turn to eat. This custom is often ignored and is now virtually non-existent in some big cities. It was believed that any leftover *laba* porridge was a good omen, as it suggested an annual surplus, and that giving away *laba* porridge to the poor was considered as a positive step in gaining good karma for the next world.

Eight-Treasure Pudding

Eight-treasured Pudding is a popular dessert to enjoy during the Spring Festival, and is usually made of sticky rice, red bean paste, sugar, and oil. The actual recipe may vary according to local variations and individual taste. In a sense, the recipe can be custom-made, and it does not necessarily require eight ingredients as the name claims. Shanghai Eight-Treasure

Eight-treasure rice pudding

Pudding, for instance, is made of longan meat, gingko, raisins, pine nuts, and melon seed meat; while its Chongqin counterpart includes lotus seeds, lily root, red dates, *yiren* (seed of Job's tears), dried tangerines, gourd slices, and honeyed cherries.

Eight-Treasure Pudding is relatively easy to make. First, rinse the sticky rice and soak it in water for 4-5 hours. Then strain the rice, spread it over the steamer covered with wet cloth, and steam it full blast uncovered until the rice turns the color of jade. After that, sprinkle on cold water to moisten the rice, and continue to steam it with the cover on for about five minutes until steam escapes from under the cover. Scoop the cooked sticky rice into a container and mix it evenly with sugar and lard, the amount of which depends on individual preferences. Grease the sides of a big bowl and spread into the bowl the prepared ingredients, then add a layer of well mixed sticky rice, followed by a layer of red bean paste, and finally more rice until the bowl is full. Place the finished product in the steamer for one more hour until the rice grains are fully expanded. Wait until the rice softens before turning the bowl upside down to empty the contents onto a plate, and then enjoy.

Eight-Treasure Pudding is colourful, sweet and deilicious. However, remember not to eat too much Eight-Treasure Pudding as it can be hard to digest.

Lanterns are displayed in celebration of the Lantern Festival

The Lantern Festival

An important traditional holiday for family reunion in China, the Lantern Festival falls on the fifteenth day of the first lunar month. That day witnesses the first full moon of the year and therefore marks the year's beginning. The Lantern Festival had its beginning in the Han Dynasty about two thousand years ago. On that day sacrifices were made to honor

Lanterns are displayed in celebration of the Lantern Festival.

Heaven, and prayers were uttered for prosperity in the earthly world. Today, the Lantern Festival is observed for good luck.

A popular saying tells us that the fifteenth day of the first lunar month should be celebrated with "a lot of noise"— i.e., with a lot of celebration including such activities as observing the moon, watching lanterns, solving lantern riddles, setting off firecrackers, and eating *tangyuan*, or dumplings.

Following in the immediate wake of the Spring Festival, the Lantern Festival is seen as its continuation as well as its conclusion.

The Lantern Festival Celebration

Lighting and Watching Lanterns

The Lantern Festival is known as the *Yuanxiao* Festival, and there are a number of different stories which explain its origin. One version is attributed to primitive people's worship of fire. As early as the Han Dynasty, people used torches to start fires in fields to drive away insects and animals. This practice later evolved into the Torch Festival, and in the Tang Dynasty into the Lantern Festival, which kicked off large-scale celebratory activities.

Prior to the Lantern Festival, around the thirteenth day of the first lunar month, shops and stores start to display colorful lanterns for sale. The following day is set aside for rehearsal. On the fifteenth day, lantern fairs are held at which the most gorgeous lanterns can be seen. Different types of lanterns in a number of colors are displayed to attract large crowds, such as imperial lanterns formerly used in palaces, rabbit-shaped lanterns, and rotating lanterns featuring galloping horses.

Dragon Dance

The dragon dance is an integral part of any celebration.

People are watching different kinds of lanterns at the Lantern Festival.

Dragon dancers are performing in celebration of the Lantern Festival.

The Spring Festival, the Lantern Festival and other major events never fail to feature a performance of the dragon dance. The dragon dance was first performed during the Song Dynasty for the dual purpose of celebrating and requesting more rain.

Dragons come in a wide variety. The most common dragons are made from bamboo with the bare structure shaped like a long hollow tunnel. Poles for gripping are installed at regular sections. The structure becomes a cloth dragon when it is wrapped in brightly-colored cloth, and becomes a dragon lantern when candles are lit inside. Other dragons include "Hundred-Leafed Dragons" constructed by weaving bamboo into the shape of a butterfly, "Bench Dragons" which are made up of a number of benches, and "Straw Dragons" which are made by tying bundles of straw together.

To perform the dragon dance requires special skills, because the longest dragon can be up to 50 - 60 meters in length, with the dragon head held between 2 and 3 meters above the ground. Only a skilled team can make the dragon dance in a graceful and breathtaking manner.

Solving riddles is an important part of the Lantern Festival celebration.

Lantern Riddles

It is common in China to hold lantern riddle fairs where participants can have fun and test their intelligence by deciphering riddles.

Riddles are pasted on the lanterns. In an effort to show off their learning, scholars in the past would compose entertaining riddles which were to be displayed on the night of the festival to draw large crowds of spectators.

Food Enjoyment

Yuanxiao

The custom of eating *yuanxiao* in celebration of the Lantern Festival dates back to the Song Dynasty. *Yuanxiao* are also called dumplings. They are so called because the round white dumplings swimming in the bowl resemble the moon which shines brightly on the fifteenth day of the first lunar month. In the past, these dumplings were only available during the Yuanxiao Festival which is how they aquired their name.

Nowadays, *yuanxiao* are no longer available only during the Lantern Festival. Frozen *yuanxiao* are available at all major supermarkets, while fresh *yuanxiao* made on the spot are served in many *dim sum* restaurants.

Yuanxiao are made of ground sticky rice, and are also sometimes stuffed with other fillings. Solid *yuanxiao* are served in fermented glutinous rice soup or sweet soup, while stuffed *yuanxiao* are usually cooked in boiling water. *Yuanxiao* recipes and flavors vary considerably from region to region. Take Beijing *yuanxiao* for instance. The first step is to prepare the filling, which is usually sweet. This is molded into small dices and then placed in a large bamboo tray covered with dry ground sticky rice. As the tray swings, they catch a layer of pulverized rice. Then they are taken out for moistening and put back to catch another layer

as the tray swings, over and over again until the dices grow into balls enveloped with multi-layered sticky rice. In southern China, the making of dumplings involves preparing sticky rice dough, stuffing the filling into dough dices, and molding them into balls. Fillings can be salty if prepared with fresh meat (or a combination of vegetables and meat), or sweet if prepared with sesame, red bean paste, and gingko.

People are eating *yuanxiao* at the Lantern Festival.

The Dragon Boat Festival

The Dragon Boat Festival falls on the fifth day of the fifth lunar month. Like other traditional holidays, it has a long history dating back to either the Spring and Autumn Period or the Warring States Period, roughly two thousand years ago. People of different ethnicities in various parts of China observe the Dragon Boat Festival in their own ways. For the Han ethnic group, celebration involves putting up pictures of the Ghost fighter Zhong Kui, eating salted eggs and *zongzi* (otherwise known as glutinous rice dumplings), hanging moxa and calamus, and wearing fragrant pouches. There are many arguments about the origins of the Dragon Boat Festival.

However, the two most popular legends focus on two historical figures, the poet Qu Yuan and General Wu Zixu.

Origins of the Dragon Boat Festival

Legend One

Qu Yuan was a great poet in ancient China and left a rich legacy of immortal poems like *Li Sao*, *Tian Wen* and *Nine Songs*. Qu Yuan acted as a minister to King Huai of the State of Chu in the Spring and

A statue of Qu Yuan the poet

Autumn Period. He urged the King of Chu to join forces with the State of Qi against the State of Qin, only to face a barrage of violent opposition from noblemen and other ministers. The King, believing the slanders being heaped on Qu Yuan, banished him from the capital and sent him into exile by the Yuan River and the Xiang River. It was during his exile that he composed his classic poem *Li Sao*, or *The Lament*.

In 278 BC, the Qin troops stormed the capital of Chu and conquered the state. Qu Yuan was heartbroken, seeing the tragic state his country was in, and on the fifth day of the fifth lunar month, having composed his swan song *Huai Sha*, he committed suicide by tying himself to a boulder and throwing himself into the Miluo River.

Grief-stricken over his death, people flocked to the river to pay their last respects to the great poet. Fishermen rowing on the river in search of his body took rice dumpling and eggs with them in the hope of feeding him. This was the start of the custom of holding Dragon Boat races and eating glutinous rice dumplings on the fifth day of the fifth lunar month. The Dragon Boat Festival is also known as the Poets' Day.

Legend Two

Like his fellow countryman Qu Yuan, General Wu Zixu was a native of the State of Chu in the Spring and Autumn Period (770 BC to 476 BC). After his father and brothers had been murdered by the King of Chu, General Wu fled his native country to seek refuge in the State of Wu, and helped the King of Wu launch a punitive war on Chu, fighting a total of five fierce battles. Finally, the Wu troops succeeded in storming the capital of Chu. By then, the King of Chu was already dead. General Wu removed the former king's corpse from his grave and subjected it to three hundred lashes to avenge his father and brothers. Upon the death of the King of Wu, his son succeeded to the throne. The Wu army then defeated the troops of the State of Yue, and forced the humiliated king to plea for peace. General Wu urged the new King of Wu to show his enemy no mercy. However, the King turned down General Wu's advice and instead handed Gernea Wu a

People are buying moxa and calamus at the Dragon Boat Festival.

sword and orderd him to take his own life, based on trumped-up charges. General Wu had no other choice. After his death, his body was wrapped in leather and thrown into a river on the fifth day of the fifth lunar month. Condqeuntly, some people argue that the Dragon Boat Festival is observed in memory of General Wu Zixu.

The Dragon Boat Festival Celebration

Hanging moxa and calamus

The Dragon Boat Festival falls on the fifth day of the fifth lunar month when the weather is beginning to turn warm, and moxa and calamus are hung at this time.

The stem and leaves of moxa, also known as Chinese mugwort,

A dragon boat race is going on in celebration of the Dragon Boat Festival.

contain a volatile aromatic substance, and its special aroma repels mosquitoes and flies. Moxa is used as an important herb in acupuncture and moxibustion (a form of heat therapy).

Calamus is a perennial aquatic plant which also contains volatile aromatic oil which stimulates the mind and kills insects. It is therefore hung in doorways and inside rooms to prevent disease and kill germs.

Dragon Boat Race

A very important part of the Dragon Boat Festival is the Dragon Boat race, which is associated with the poet Qu Yuan. When the poet committed suicide by throwing himself into the river, boats hastily flocked to the scene and vied with each other in an intense search for his body, though they found no trace of it. Since then, Dragon Boat races have been held to cherish the memory of this great poet.

The Dragon Boat race is a widely popular sport which also found its way to Japan, Vietnam and other

There is a large selection of colorful fragrant pouches.

neighboring countries. Races are held every year in various parts of China. In 1980, the Dragon Boat race was officially included in national athletic games and sports tournaments. Since then, the annual nationwide Dragon Boat race has been held under the title of "Qu Yuan Cup".

Wearing Fragrant Pouches

In some parts of China, children are made to wear fragrant pouches for the Dragon Boat Festival. The pouches are stuffed with spices and herbs, taking the shape of animals or of a miniature heart. They are worn to dispel evil spirits and ward off diseases at the time of year when insects begin to thrive and spread diseases.

As they are often exquisitely made, fragrant pouches can be worn on the clothes as a decoration. At City God Temple in Shanghai, a famous tourist attraction, there is a large selection of colorful fragrant pouches to choose from.

Food Enjoyment

Zongzi or Rice Dumplings

Rice dumplings are made by wrapping glutinous rice and fillings tightly

Zongzi, otherwise known as rice dumplings.

in bamboo leaves and then simmered in water. They are shaped like pyramids, bed pillows, or a woman's bound feet, a common sight in feudal China.

The practice of eating rice dumplings originated in the Eastern Han Dynasty and was limited to certain geographical areas. That it turned into a tradition with gaining popularity was attributed to the death of Qu Yuan. Legend has it that on the Dragon Boat Festival large quantities of rice dumplings were dumped in the river where the poet had taken his own life to scare away fish and shrimp so that they would not feed on the poet's body, in the hope that it could be kept intact. Although the tale is no longer much talked about, the delicious rice dumplings have been preserved to this day.

As China is a vast country, taste preferences differ wildly between the north and the south. Rice dumplings in northern China have an impressive size while those in southern China, with the exception of Hainan Island, are relatively small. Rice dumplings in the north are sweet while those in the south are often salty.

The best known rice dumplings in the north are those made in Beijing, which are large, three- or four-cornered, and filled with red dates and red bean paste, sometimes

A foreigner is learning to wrap *zongzi*.

Zongzi is a popular delicacy.

with preserved fruits or meats.

The best loved rice dumplings in the south are those made in Guangdong and Jiaxing, Zhejiang. Guangdong rice dumplings may be small but they are renowned for their variety, and include red bean paste *zongzi*, pork *zongzi*, chicken *zongzi*, duck *zongzi*, barbecued pork *zongzi*, and mushroom *zongzi*. Sometimes, salted egg yolk is added to generate a deeper flavor. Jiaxing rice dumplings are nationally known, especially those that bear the brand name of Wufangzhai, which are famous for the choice ingredients they use. Wufangzhai rice dumplings, with a tempting aroma and flavor, are a very popular specialty.

In the past, on the fifth day of the fifth lunar month, housewives were kept occupied cleaning bamboo leaves in water, soaking glutinous rice, and wrapping rice dumplings. Nowadays, most people, especially city-dwellers, are too busy to make their own rice dumplings, and content themselves with those from supermarkets or restaurants. Today, fewer and fewer people are skilled at wrapping rice dumplings. Those who can do this well are usually advanced in age.

Eating Five-Yellow Meals

In regions near the Yangtze River delta, there is an unusual custom called "eating a five-yellow meal". These five yellow foods are eel, yellow fish, cucumber, salted egg yolk, and realgar wine. The most opportune time for eating such a meal is the middle of the day. According to traditional Chinese medicine, the *yang* force is at its strongest on the fifth day of the fifth lunar month, and particularly so in the middle of that day.

The five-yellow meal is so scheduled as to capitalize on the *yang* force which negates bad fortune and invigorates the body.

The above five-yellow meal combination is by no means universal. In some places, it may consist of yellow fish, cucumber, egg yolk, soy beans, and day lily, depending on availability.

Realgar wine is a poisonous wine, and is known as *xionghuang* in China. Mild and bitter, it contains arsenic sulfide from which white arsenic is extracted. According to traditional Chinese medicine, external use of realgar can cure skin diseases, swellings, and snake and insect bites. Internal use though a micro dosage is said to cure epilepsy and sores. Because of its highly toxic nature, oral use of realgar is restricted and highly dangerous. It is a misconception to assume that realgar wine can liquidate toxins and dispel evil. Modern scientific research has proven that realgar contains a strong cancer-inducing substance and may cause hepatic damage even if administered orally in micro dosages. Symptoms range from nausea, vomiting, and diarrhea to dysfunction of the central nerve system, unconsciousness, coma and even death. Therefore, these days rice wine is substituted for realgar wine in this meal.

Chinese rice wine is one of the oldest brewed alcohols in the wolrd, and the alcohol content of rice wine can reach 15 degrees. It is made from grains. In southern China, plain rice is generally used as the raw ingredient to be brewed into wine. However, the best ingredient is glutinous rice. Rice wine does not necessarily appear yellow; it can be black or red. Rice wine is mellow, fragrant, refreshing, and the taste ranges from sweet to mildl. The best-known rice wine in China is manufactured in Shaoxing, Zhejiang Province.

Chinese Valentine's Day

Valentines' Day in Western countries occurs on February 14 of each year, while Chinese Valentine's Day falls on the seventh day of the seventh lunar month.

This traditional holiday is related to a fascinating romantic folk tale. There was once an orphaned boy who was an oxherd. He toiled all day long and his only company was an old ox. To put an end to his solitude, the old ox thought out a plan to persuade a fairy called the Weaving Maid to marry the oxherd.

One day, a group of beautiful fairies were bathing in the Milky Way. The oxherd, who had been hiding and watching them, ran off with the Weaving Maid's robes. Seeing this, all the fairies hastily put on their own clothes and fled the scene, leaving the Weaving Maid on her own. The oxherd then approached her and asked her to marry him, to which she agreed. After the marriage, their mutual affection knew no bounds. They bore children, and built a happy home. However, their marriage had aroused the wrath of the Jade Emperor and Empress Huang Mu, who sent celestial generals down to the earth to capture the Weaving Maid while her husband was away. Seeing his wife gone, the oxherd followed them in hot pursuit. Empress Huang Mu took her gold hairpin and waved at to the Milky Way like a magic wand. Suddenly, turbulent raging waters

The Oxherd and the Weaving Maid reunite each year on the seventh day of the seventh lunar month.

arose on the placid surface of the Milky Way, forcing the oxherd to give up his chase. Separated by the waters, the couple could only look at each other from the riverbanks, with tears in their eyes. However, their strong love touched the Emperor and the Empress, who eventually relented and allowed them to meet once a year on the seventh day of the seventh lunar month. On that day, countless magpies fly into the sky and convert themselves into a bridge stretched across the Milky Way to make the lovers' reunion possible. The phrase "meeting on the magpie bridge" was thus coined to refer to seeking true love.

Chinese Valentine's Day occurs as summer drifts into autumn. It is a time when the sky is filled with a multitude of twinkling stars at night. The two brightest stars opposite each other are seen to represent the Oxherd and the Weaving Maid. The legendary Weaving Maid is thought to be beautiful and dexterous, with a heart of gold. On Chinese Valentine's night, women ask to be blessed with her intelligence, her superb craft skills and a perfect marriage. Chinese Valentine is therefore also known as "Craft Skills Day" or "Women's Day".

The Mid-Autumn Festival

The Mid-Autumn Festival falls on the fifteenth day of the eighth lunar month. This ancient holiday is so called because it occurs halfway through autumn.

Like the Spring Festival, the Mid-Autumn Festival is regarded as an occasion for family reunion. On that day, the moon is supposed to be nearest to the earth and can be seen at its fullest and brightest. On this day, families often gather for a feast, which includes moon cakes and seasonal fruits, while observing the moon. People who cannot be near their family at this time also look up to the moon, which reminds them of their home.

The Mid-Autumn Festival is no longer only celebrated by the Han ethnic group, but is enjoyed throughout China. The character "mid-autumn" appeared for the first time in *Zhou Li*, written in the Warring States Period. In other words, the holiday was recorded as early as 2,000 years ago, but it did not become a holiday of national importance until the Tang Dynasty.

According to legend, the Mid-Autumn Festival came about because ancient emperors offered a sacrifice to the moon in autumn. It was customary in ancient time that emperors should, through sacrificial ceremonies, worship the sun in spring and the moon in fall. Gradually, worshipping the moon gave way to observing the moon, and the tedious ceremony to fun activities.

Origins of the Mid-Autumn Festival

Legend One

In ancient time there were ten suns in the sky, whose combined intense heat scorched and parched the earth, causing crop failures, devastation and sufferings. A man named Houyi decided to end this havoc for the benefit of the common people. He scaled the peak of Kunlun Mountain and shot down nine of the suns with his giant bow. He then ordered the one remaining sun to rise in the morning and set in the evening.

Houyi's wife, whose name was Chang'e, was beautiful and kind. The couple were devoted to each other and led a happy life. One day, on his way to Kunlun Mountain for a visit to his friend, Houyi bumped into an immortal god and obtained from him some longevity pills which, once swallowed, would enable him to also become an immortal and ascend to Heaven. Despite his strong desire to be an immortal, Houyi could not tear himself away from his loving wife. So he left the pills in his wife's care.

Three days later, while Houyi was away on a hunting trip, a man called Pengmeng broke into his house, sword in hand, demanding the longevity pills from Chang'e. Chang'e was worried, and the only thing she could think of doing was to swallow the pills herself to stop Pengmeng from getting hold of them. When she did so, she suddenly

became a fairy and flew up into
the sky, but she stopped to land
on the moon, the nearest satellite
of the Earth, so that she would
not be too far from her husband.

Returning home and having
heard the maid's account of the
event, Houyi was overwhelmed
with grief and brought out his
wife's favorite fruit and cakes
into the garden and presented
them to her. That night, the moon
was especially full and bright.
The event had occurred on the
fifteenth day of the eighth lunar
month. When the local villagers
came to learn what had happened to Chang'e, they likewise set up altars
under the moon to pray for peace and good luck from the kind-hearted
woman. Gradually, the custom of worshipping the moon during the Mid-
Autumn Festival took root.

The Mid-Autumn Festival celebrations.

Legend Two

On the moon there was said to be a palace called the Grand Moon
Palace, in front of which stood a huge laurel tree with luxuriant foliage.
Every day, a woodcutter came to prune the tree, only to find the tree full
of twigs as before. The chopping thus went on for ever and the man's

toil ended up in nothing. Wu Gong, for that was the woodcutter's name, was a native of Xihe during the Han Dynasty. He had once followed an immortal to cultivate himself. However, because of an error he had committed, he had been banished to the moon as a punishment. On the moon he was destined to continuously do the same work in attempting to prune the laurel tree in front of the Grand Moon Palace.

The Mid-Autumn Festival is the time for narrating all kinds of stories about the moon, none of them necessarily related to the origin of the festival. Since the festival was rooted in the worship of the moon, discussion of legends about the moon are naturally inseparable from the Mid-Autumn Festival.

Food Enjoyment

Moon Cakes

The Mid-Autumn Festival celebration is not complete without eating moon cakes. These were originally offered as a sacrifice to the moon, and were later eaten while observing the moon on the Mid-Autumn Festival, and have therefore become a symbol of family reunion.

The custom of eating moon cakes came into existence during the Yuan Dynasty and is associated with Zhu Yuanzhang, the leader of the peasants' uprising. In order to shake off the shackle of the tyrannical rule of Yuan Dynasty, rebellions erupted all over central China. Zhu Yuanzhang tried to co-ordinate the scattered rebel forces into a united uprising. However, he could not find a suitable means of communication to transmit his messages, because of the strict control of the imperial

Moon cakes

government. Zhu's military adviser hit on a good idea. A secret message was to be embedded inside the moon cakes, stating that "the uprising was scheduled for the night of the fifteenth day of the eighth lunar month". When the moon cakes were delivered to the rebel forces, the message was received. The rebel forces launched a joint action on the scheduled date, marched into the capital of the Yuan Dynasty, and won the final victory. The story of this brilliant tactic began to circulate among the general population who then started the custom of making and giving away moon cakes as gifts.

Due to geographical differences, the shape, texture, and method of baking moon cakes varies throughout the country. They come in different local styles, such as Guangdong style, Suzhou style, Chaozhou style, Beijing style, Ningbo style, and Yunnan style. Beijing-style moon cakes are perfectly suited for vegetarians, Guangdong-style moon cakes contain a little oil and a lot of sugar, Suzhou-style moon cakes are filled with a lot of both oil and sugar, while Chaozhou-style moon cakes contain crunchy sugar.

Today, the most common and best-loved moon cakes are those made in the Guangdong style, known for their high-quality ingredients and unique preparation process. The convex patterns on the coverings are easily identifiable, and Guangdong-style moon cakes are tender, rich, and heavy, with thin crusts and thick fillings.

Taro and Green Soy Beans

In areas south of the Yangtze River, it is popular to eat taro and green soy beans in addition to moon cakes at the Mid-Autumn Festival. These two vegetables ripen around the middle of the eighth lunar month. Initially used for sacrificial purposes, they are have now become part of local traditions. Taro can be cooked with green onions and oil and served as a salty dish. It can also be cooked as a sweet dish, such as laurel-flavored sweet taro soup or soft boiled taro covered with sugar and shredded laurel petal. These are popular with people in southern China who usually have a sweet tooth. Green soy beans, meanwhile, are normally served as a side dish. However, at the Mid-Autumn Festival, they enjoy an elevated status. The two ends having been clipped off, they are boiled in salt water with their shells intact and enjoyed as a main dish.

Moon cake sales show a huge increase around the time of the Mid-Autumn Festival. Most of them are intended as gifts for friends and relatives. Moon cakes should be eaten sparingly because of their high-sugar and high-fat content. In today's China, moon cakes are treated as a symbol of luck and reunion. The exchange of moon cakes as gifts shows a desire to look forward to happiness and prosperity.

The Mid-Autumn Festival Celebration

The Mid-Autumn Festival is celebrated differently according to local customs in different parts of China.

In addition to moon cakes, people in Nanjing eat "laurel duck". This particular breed of duck reaches its maturity at the same time that laurel trees burst into blossom and release their distinctive fragrance, and hence they are known as "laurel ducks". Tasty and delicious, "laurel duck" is a specialty in Nanjing.

In Sichuan, people observe the holiday by eating duck, sesame cakes and honey cakes, and by lighting orange lanterns, which are made by placing small candles inside hollowed oranges.

In Guangdong, people make water lanterns which float on the rivers to please the River God. These create a sea of moving lights with the reflection of the moon serving as the backdrop, creating a beautiful scene.

In Hong Kong, people give performances of the Fire Dragon Dance on the night before the Mid-Autumn Festival, mostly in Tong Lo Wan, or Causeway Bay. The Fire Dragon is made of bundles of straw covered with sticks of burning incense. At night, as the Fire Dragon rolls, jumps, and plunges, large crowds of spectators watch in awe.

Customs of the Mid-Autumn Festival celebration vary from place to place. Most customs are being slowly becoming neglected, with the exception of observing the moon while eating moon cakes.

The Moon on the Mid-Autumn Festival

The moon is at its brightest during the Mid-Autumn Festival every year. It is often described as "white and luminous" at this time. As a matter of fact, the moon never fails to appear full on the fifteenth day of every lunar month. How does it come about that the moon looks its brightest on the fifteenth day of the eighth lunar month?

The full moon is shining bright on the night of the Mid-Autumn Festival.

According to Chinese meteorologists, the dry and cold air currents sweeping from the north at that time drive southward the warm and moist currents hovering over most of China throughout the summer, thus thinning the clouds. Meanwhile, due to the increased leaning angle of the sun, the earth is exposed to less sunshine and heat, which means that the resultant temperature is much lower. As moisture in the air decreases due to the dry winter wind, visibility increases. As a result, autumn weather is mild and crisp, the sky is high, and the night sky is cloudless and clear. That explains why the moon looks particularly bright during the Mid-Autumn Festival.

Climbing mountains is a popular event at the Double Ninth Festival.

The Double Ninth Festival

On the ninth day of the ninth lunar month is a traditional holiday called the Double Ninth Festival. It is so called because in ancient China, six was defined as a *yin* number and nine as a *yang* number, and that particular day represents two nines and consequently two *yang*.

The Double Ninth Festival occurs in the autumn when the harvest is in sight and rejoicing is widespread. The Chinese love to use homophones, and "nine" sounds exactly the same as "prolonged" in Chinese. Moreover, nine is the biggest single digit number. Therefore, Double Ninth suggests "a prolonged life" or longevity. In 1989, the ninth day of the ninth lunar month was designated as the Senior Citizens' Day, a special day on which the elderly are shown reverence, respect, love, and care.

Every year on the Double Ninth Festival, activities are conducted in various parts of China to entertain the elderly.

The Double Ninth Festival Celebration

Scaling Heights

"Scaling heights", more commonly known as mountain-climbing, is a popular activity on the Double Ninth Festival, and it is therefore sometimes also known as the "Mountain-Climbing Day". This custom dates back to the Eastern Han Dynasty. Since then, climbing hills and mountains in groups has been a popular way to celebrate the Double Ninth Festival. The autumen weather, with crisp air and clear skies, provides a perfect environment for this

Chrysanthemums are swaying in the breeze.

activity. Looking down on the world from a high summit, one is sure to be filled with a sense of exhilaration. Mountain-climbing has gained popularity because it symbolizes not only longevity but also ambition and a strong will.

Watching Chrysanthemums

Chrysanthemums are in full bloom by the ninth day of the ninth lunar month. It is a perfect season, as far as ancient scholars were concerned, for watching chrysanthemums, drinking chrysanthemum wine, and composing expressive and emotive poems. The practice of watching chrysanthemums and drinking chrysanthemum wine is said to have originated with Tao Yuanming, a poet in the Jin Dynasty. Tao ended up as a hermit living in seclusion in the mountains, and he was known to have a passion for chrysanthemums. He also used to while away his time by drinking wine brewed from chrysanthemum. Soon, others began to follow his example, and today the most important part of the Double Ninth Festival celebration is the enjoyment of chrysanthemum. The ninth lunar month is also sometimes referred to as the "Chrysanthemum Month".

Wearing *Zhuyu*

Zhuyu, otherwise known as cornus officinalis, is a deciduous shrub, with oval-shaped leaves and yellow flowers. Its fruit is an oblong drupe and is a bright cherry red. On the Double Ninth Festival, women and children wear *zhuyu* on their arms or heads, or *zhuyu* fragrant pouches beneath their outer garments, in order to protect themselves against dirt and to ward off evil. Wearing *zhuyu* on the Double Ninth Festival was already a popular custom as early as the Tang Dynasty, according to historical records.

Food Enjoyment

Eating Cakes

Scaling heights on the Double Ninth Festival is a fascinating custom, but it is difficult for people living in flat cities to climb mountains or to find any heights to scale. Instead, people hit upon the ingenious idea of making cakes, since the two Chinese characters "height" and "cake" share the same pronunciation and tone. The Double Ninth Festival Cake are sometimes called flower cakes, chrysanthemum cakes, or colorless cakes. The main ingredient for making Double Ninth Festival Cakes is ground rice, mixed with walnut meat and dates. Elaborate cakes sometimes consist of nine layers like a pagoda, dotted at the top with two tiny imitations of lambs, or tiny trianglular flags. Back in the Ming and Qing Dynasties, it was customary that early in the morning on the ninth day of the ninth lunar month, a Double Ninth Festival Cake would be cut into flaky slices to be pasted on children's foreheads as a blessing

Double Ninth Festival cake.

to ensure that their life would be satisfactory and that their future careers would be successful.

Drinking Chrysanthemum Wine

Chrysanthemum used as a tonic is known for its vitality and energy and as such it is often used to celebrate longevity. Chrysanthemum wine represents good fortune. It is made by brewing grain mixed with chrysanthemum picked on the Double Ninth Festival — the wine is usually set aside for one year until the next Double Ninth Festival. Chrysanthemum wine is said to stimulate eyesight, invigorate the liver, pacify the stomach, reduce elevated blood pressure, and generally promote good health.

The Chinese Zodiac

The Chinese lunar calendar uses ten heavenly stems and twelve earthly branches to record the year, month, day and hour. The Chinese zodiac signs, consisting of twelve animals, correspond to the twelve earthly branches.

In colloquial terms, the Chinese zodiac refers to the twelve animals representing different years. Twelve specific animals are singled out to record time, with twelve years as a cycle. The animal representing the year of an individual's birth becomes his or her zodiac animal. The twelve animals appear in a slightly different sequence, according to different ethnic groups. For instance, for the Han ethnic group, the sequence is rat, ox, tiger, rabbit, dragon, snake, horse, sheep (or goat), monkey, rooster, dog, and pig (or boar). However, for the Mongolian ethnic group, the sequence is tiger, rabbit, dragon, snake, horse, sheep (or goat), monkey, rooster, dog, and pig (or boar), rat, and ox.

The origin of the Chinese zodiac is explained in different ways. Some argue that it can be traced to time immemorial. Zhao Yi, a scholar in the Qing Dynasty, believed that it had originated with the nomadic tribes in northern China. Modern Chinese scholars, headed by the renowned Guo Moro, contend that it came from Babylonia. However, a large amount of data provided by experts based on years of research has revealed that Chinese zodiac was indigenous to China and was a combination of early

Paper cuttings of twelve zodiac animals

Chinese animal worship, totem worship, and astrology.

In spite of these different schools of thoughts, competing folk tales and myths about the origin of Chinese zodiac have become ingrained in different areas.

Origin of the Chinese Zodiac

One story states that long ago, early one morning, the Venerable God of the Golden Star hurried to the Heavenly Palace for an audience with the Jade Emperor. He reported: "I descended to the earthly world the other day and discovered that there was no calendar, no division of seasons, and no senior or junior ranking system among the people there. Their world is full of confusion and complaints, so something must be done to solve this situation."

The Jade Emperor asked "What is your solution?" The Venerable God of the Golden Star replied: "We could recruit twelve animals to Heaven as zodiac representations and involve them in the task of recording the hour, the day, and the year. This would help the people on earth understand the passage of time."

The Jade Emperor nodded his consent. The Venerable God of the Golden Star thus hired twelve animals and set up the zodiac representations.

Chinese Zodiac Culture

The creation of the Chinese zodiac brought about an excellent opportunity for artistic creation. Over the past thousands of years, fine works of art which relate to the Chinese zodiac have been created. For example, Tang Dynasty bronze mirros are very popular for their detailed zodiac designs and exquisite workmanship. Other works include zodiac paper cuttings which are an ancient traditional art, and zodiac New Year posters which combine zodiac animals and human characters to create a vivid and playful effect, and therefore serve as popular festival decorations.

The most popular zodiac-related objects in contemporary China are Chinese zodiac stamps. Every year on February 5 the Chinese Post Service puts out stamps bearing the zodiac animal of the year. As it is popular to buy those stamps on the first day of sale, stamp collectors rise early to queue up in front of the post offices, which shows the tremendous popularity of Chinese zodiac stamps.

The Vulnerable Year

The vulnerable year is a very important concept in the Chinese zodiac. The reoccurrence of the lunar year in which a person's birth occurs is called their vulnerable year. For instance, if someone was born in 2006, the year of the dog, the reappearance of the year of the dog marks his or her vulnerable year. Since Chinese zodiac runs in a cycle of twelve, the vulnerable year occurs once every twelve years.

The vulnerable year is commonly believed to be an ominous year. But such a belief remains to be accounted for. In the past, people believed that everyone, from emperors, kings, ministers and generals down to workers

Wearing red is encouraged in a person's "vulnerable" year.

and peasants, is bound to be confronted with disasters at one time or another in their lives. Each vulnerable year is, therefore, a stumbling block in the voyage of life. Since the vulnerable year is considered ominous, something must be done to avert disasters.

Red is seen as a auspicious color, and it is therefore believed that wearing red is the key to averting disasters that occur in a vulnerable year. People of Han ethnicity tend to wear red sashes and red underwear. This practice used to be prevalent only in the north of China, but has recently been adopted in the south as well, particularly in metropolises like Shanghai. At the Spring Festival, people whose vulnerable year is about to begin purchase red clothes and red adornments, such as wrist chains woven with red strings, red sweaters, or red ties. Indeed, anything red may be bought, for it is commonly believed that wearing red can repel disasters.

Twenty-Four
Seasonal Division Points

Formation

Winter is filled with desolation, spring with flowers, and summer with fruits, while autumn is golden with the coming harvest.

That is how the four seasons perpetually rotate in a cycle. The formation of twenty-four seasonal division points by which the solar year is divided under the traditional Chinese calendar reveals what human beings know about nature, keeping track of the occurrence of the four seasons. China invented gunpowder, paper, printing and the compass, thereby making significant contributions to world civilization. The formation of the twenty-four points is another major milestone and exerts an impact no less than that of the "four great inventions".

By the time of the Zhou Dynasty, the Chinese people had grasped the technique of calculating the occurrence of the summer solstice, winter solstice, vernal equinox, and autumnal equinox by observing patterns of sunshine and daily shadow. The book *Huainanzi*, written in the Western Han Dynasty, contains a complete record of the twenty-four seasonal division points, which have since played an essential role in guiding and regulating life and production.

The twenty-four points are determined by the location of the earth in its orbit around the sun. It takes 365 days for the earth to complete a single orbit around the sun. The ancient Chinese divided 360 degrees by 24, designating *chunfen* (vernal equinox) at 0 degree and *qingming* (clear and bright) at 15 degrees, followed by a different solar term at every 15 degrees. These were *lichun* (the beginning of spring), *yushui* (rain water), *jingzhe* (the awakening of insects), *chunfen* (the vernal equinox), *qingming* (clear and bright), *guyu* (grain rains), *lixia*, (the start of summer), *xiaoman* (grain full), *mangzhong* (grain in ear), *xiazhi* (the summer solstice), *xiaoshu* (minor heat), *dashu* (major heat*)*, *liqiu* (the start of autumn), *chushu* (the limit of heat), *bailu* (white dew), *qiufen* (the autumnal equinox), *hanlu* (cold dew), *shuangjiang* (the descent of frost), *lidong* (the start of winter), *xiaoxue* (*minor* snow), *daxue* (*major* snow), *dongzhi* (the winter solstice) and *xiaohan* (minor cold), *dahan* (major cold).

The twenty-four points reflect the different positions of the sun in its orbit as well as the seasonal rotation, and also record the occurrence of climatic phenomena in nature, which had a far-reaching impact on agricultural production. For instance, at *jingzhe*, slumbering insects are sure to awaken at the roar of thunder; in spring, trees begin to sprout and it is consequentially time to plant rice and cotton; and at *qingming*, spring rain is sure to sprinkle over the areas south of the Yangtze River. The twenty-four seasonal division points therefore accurately forecast the occurrence of happenings in nature.

The twenty-four points occur on relatively fixed calendar days as

Flowers are in bloom, braving the heavy snow.

follows: the 5th or 6th and 21st in the first half of the year and the 8th and 23rd in the second half, with two solar terms occurring every month.

The Twenty-Four Seasonal Division Points

Lichun (The Beginning of Spring)

Li means start or beginning, and *Lichun* therefore means the start of spring. It signals the approach of warm weather and the revival of nature. *Lichun* occurs during the Spring Festival.

The term *Lichun* is different from the word for spring that is used in the meteorological sense. *Lichun* occurs around February every year when the climate is still frigid and spring in the true sense of the word is yet to come. In late March, as more warm and comfortable weather sets in, trees grow leaves and flowers blossom. Therefore, *Lichun* is more correctly the harbinger of spring.

Lichun is the time when cold and warm air currents begin to repel each other, causing considerable fluctuations in temperature. It often happens that while it is sunny and bright in the middle of the day, a cold air current may suddenly descend in the evening, with gusts of chilly wind more reminiscent of winter. This caprice is known as "reversed spring chill" which poses a high risk for the elderly suffering from hypertension, stroke, and heart disease.

Yushui (Rain Water)

Yushui follows immediately in the wake of Lichun and occurs in the second half of February. Taking the word in its literal sense, it is obvious that more and more rain water is on the way. Before the arrival of yushui, the temperature is generally around freezing. The Yellow River areas are still filled with snow while southern China suffers a scarcity of rain. After *yushui* sets in, the average temperature in southern China approaches 10 degrees Celsius and plants begin to show signs of life. At this time, the temperature in the Yellow River areas goes above 0 degree Celsius and ice slowly begins to thaw.

Jingzhe (The Awakening of Insects)

Zhefu is a Chinese term that denotes a hibernating animal which neither moves nor feeds. But when the word *zhe* is used in conjunction with *jing*, the resultant phrase has the connotation of awakening a sleeping animal or insect.

In nature, the only thing that awakens a hibernating animal is thunder. *Jingzhe* occurs at the beginning of March and signals the approach of a warmer climate. Spring is now increasingly making itself felt and roaring thunder may strike at any time to awaken all the hibernating animals from their long winter sleep.

In China, *jingzhe* marks the beginning of the ploughing season. A popular saying states "On with spring ploughing after *jingzhe*." This expression summarizes the Chinese farmers' experience based on traditional farming routines. Weather in the *jingzhe* period is highly changeable and it pays to check the daily weather report to determine what to wear for the day.

Chunfen (The Vernal Equinox)

Chunfen occurs in the second half of March. What is special about *chunfen* is that its nights and days are of equal length. Out of the twenty-four points in a year, only two share this phenomenon: *chunfen* (the vernal equinox) and *qiufen* (the autumnal equinox). After *chunfen*, the days grow longer and the nights shorter until the summer solstice occurs.

Chunfen is a sign of the start of a more agreeable and serene season. Farmers start planting paddy seedlings, corn and trees. The countryside is usually full of life and vitality at this time. During the *chunfen* period, southern China is likely to be hit by cold spells. Therefore, it is necessary to be careful to stay warm.

Qingming (Clear and Bright)

Qingming occurs at the beginning of April. The Chinese treat *qingming* as a holiday, named the Clear and Bright Festival. In April, nature is back to life and the land is a vast stretch of green. After a long and monotonous winter, people cannot wait to take trips in such agreeable weather. Therefore, the Clear and Bright Festival is also known as the Excursion Festival. Clear and Bright has two different concepts as a holiday and as a seasonal division point. The former is a festival marked by various folk

Left: The busy tea picking season sets in around the Qingming period.

activities, while the latter is simply a seasonal and climatic marker.

Qingming is the time for offering sacrifice to ancestors and cherishing memories of deceased friends and relatives by paying respects at their gravesites. In the past, visiting gravesites was a burdensome affair which not only involved bringing fruits, cakes, cooked dishes, and wine, but also involved loosening the soil around graves, planting fresh twigs, burning paper money, and kowtowing. However, these rituals are no longer being followed with as much fervor as before. Nowadays, city dwellers usually bring bouquets of flowers and make bows in honor of the departed. Offering fresh cooked food is no longer popular and burning paper money is usually restricted to rural areas.

A good deal of rainfall occurs during the *qingming* period, and that year's tea begins to be available on the market. In areas south of the Yangtze River, tea is divided into two kinds, based on the time of picking: pre-*qingming* tea and post-*qingming* tea. The former is picked and processed between 1 and 30 days before *qingming*, and the latter after *qingming*. The general belief is that the earliest of that year's tea available on the market is the best quality, because in early spring tea shrubs generate fewer leaves, which are therefore time-consuming to pick and difficult to process. That explains why pre-*qingming* tea is highly priced. Take the famous Lion Peak, a brand of Dragon Well tea. It costs anywhere from 3,000 RMB to 4,000 RMB per kilogram. Post-*qingming* tea is considered to be common and is sold at a much lower price.

Guyu (Grain Rains)

Guyu occurs around the 20th of April when abundant rain begins to benefit the growing of grain crops. The name *guyu* suggests that rain helps to speed up crop growth. At this time, farmers get ready for the planting season. In areas south of the Yangtze River, the planting of rice and cotton occurs during this period. Any delay would result in having no crops at all. In northern China, the planting and subsequent sprouting of spring crops also takes place in this period.

In southern China, it is during the *guyu* period that peonies, the Chinese national flower, burst into blossom. For this reason, the peony is also called the *guyu* flower.

Lixia (The Beginning of Summer)

As the term indicates, lixia means the start of summer. It occurs around the 6th of May. However, *lixia* is merely a seasonal marker and one should not be misled into believing that summer has arrived. Summer is considered to begin only when the average temperature exceeds 22 degrees Celsius for five consecutive days.

China is of continental proportion and is made up of diverse terrains, which explains the climatic polarization between southern and northern China. The climatic difference reflected at *lixia* is distinct. While it may be summer in some southernmost parts of China, it is still late spring in many northern areas.

At *lixia*, crops grow quickly. Whether rain comes early or not and whether it comes in large or scarce quantities constitute decisive factors in determining the scale of the year's harvest.

Summer is the hottest season of the year. In order to withstand intense heat, people pay particular attention to their diet. Low-fat, low-salt, and high-fiber food is preferred at this time of year. It is also customary to eat eggs at the height of summer, purportedly to strengthen the body and the stomach and to enable a person to walk in firm vigorous steps, since an old proverb tells us: "Eat eggs at *lixia* and stone slabs will break under your steps."

After *lixia*, the temperature increases daily to the extent of causing physical discomfort, loss of appetite, and weight loss. These symptoms are collectively known as "summer syndrome". The key to preventing this, it is said, is by eating eggs.

There are many different popular ways of eating eggs. One is to boil the eggs in water, shell them, and cook them in a soup with red dates. Another is to cook the eggs in boiling water, dye the shells with red rice, and put them in small nets to be worn around children's necks to be eaten in the afternoon. Eggs are generally believed to strengthen the body and the stomach.

Xiaoman (Grain Full)

Xiaoman occurs on the 20th or 21st of May, which is the optimum time for planting paddy seedlings. It is also the ripening season for summer crops like horse beans and wheat. The character *man* refers to the flooding of a field. Lack of water leads to parched soil which makes rice growing impossible, so a popular saying notes that "A flooded paddy field promises a full granary. A drop of water conserved is a grain of rice ensured." Therefore, water conservation is of great importance in the *xiaoman* period.

Mangzhong (Grain Ear)

Mangzhong marks the period when wheat is ready to burst into ears

Wheat is being cut manually.

and ripen. It is a season for both harvesting and planting. Farmers are busily engaged in cutting wheat and planting rice. This hectic season is also known as the season of "summer harvest and summer planting."

In areas south of the Yangtze River, *Mangzhong* signals the start of the monsoons, referred to locally as plum rain. They are so called because they coincide with the ripening of plums. Due to excessive rain and sultry weather condition, indoor objects and belongings are liable to get moldy, hence the other name of "moldy rain". During this period, rainy weather and clear weather alternate, causing low air pressure which contributes to bodily discomforts, especially to those suffering from heart complaints. The idea of a trip to southern provinces at this time should be brushed aside.

Xiazhi (The Summer Solstice)

Xiazhi occurs on the 21st or 22nd of June when the day is the longest and the night the shortest in the northern hemisphere. The sun's vertical position happens to be at the northernmost on this day, almost covering the Tropic of Cancer. The further north one travels, the longer daylight lasts. Take Mohe, situated on the Heilongjiang River, where daylight is as long as 17 hours on the day of *xiazhi*.

After *xiazhi*, the sun's vertical position shifts southward so that the days get shorter but the nights longer until the winter solstice, thus completing a cycle.

Xiazhi represents the true start of summer. Temperatures after *xiazhi* will gradually increase. Due to adequate sunshine, crops grow rapidly and plot management should be made a top priority.

Xiaoshu (Minor Heat)

Shu is synonymous with intense heat and *xiaoshu* suggests the start of increasingly hot weather. However, the hottest days are yet to come.

Xiaoshu occurs around the 7th of July when the sun reaches 105 degrees of ecliptic longitude. At this time, southern China is already in full summer. In some river valleys lying below sea level in southern and eastern China, it is not uncommon for the temperature to reach 35 degrees Celsius, to the detriment of the sprouting and blossoming of hybrid rice. This naturally calls for better plot management.

Around July, violent rainstorms occur in southern China. High wind and heavy precipitation contribute to natural disasters, which makes preventive measures necessary. Typhoons are likely to hit the coastal areas of southern China and the Taiwan region. It pays to remain alert.

Xiaoshu marks the start of a busy farming season. People are likely to feel run-down, listless, and easily irritable at this time. Therefore, it is necessary to pay particular attention to health by way of a controlled, wholesome and healthy diet.

Dashu (Major Heat)

Dashu occurs on the 23rd or 24th of July in the immediate wake of *xiaoshu*. As the meaning of the word indicates, the hottest days in a year occur around this period. In the middle and lower reaches of the Yangtze River where high sub-tropical air pressure holds sway, the highest temperatures can reach 37 degrees Celsius. With little wind and high humidity, the weather is often stiflingly hot.

Farmers in the two-crop rice growing areas are faced with the most hectic and daunting task of the year: to quickly harvest the early rice and also to plant the late rice. Any delay in planting the late rice would result in reduced yields, or even a failed crip. Therefore, there is a race against time as seedlings must be planted before the weather changes for the worse.

In the *dashu* period, it is unbearably hot, which affects daily life considerably. Strokes and physical discomforts are not uncommon. It is therefore of great importance to take measures to stay cool.

Liqiu (The Start of Autumn)

Liqiu signals the arrival of autumn and occurs on the 7th or 8th of August. It marks the gradual end of the sweltering summer heat. Following *liqiu*, the weather becomes cooler every day. From a meteorological point of view, autumn is considered to be around only when the average temperature remains below 22 degrees Celsius for five consecutive days.

Because of the significantly diverse climate, the entry into autumn differs from region to region. Autumn makes its appearance in mid-August in Heilongjiang and northern Xinjiang; in early September in Beijing when the autumn winds begin to blow; in mid-September in the Qinling Mountains and the Huai River areas; and in early October in Nanchang of Jiangsi Province and Hengyang of Hunan Province where the signs of autumn creep in quietly.

In fact, the temperature in most of China remains relatively high during *liqiu*. This is the time of Indian summer, and the heat is comparable to that of *dashu*. Cautionary measures therefore need to be taken to bring the heat and high temperature under control.

Great importance has always been attached to *liqiu* for farming reasons. In the *liqiu* period, crops show tremendous growth, and many start to blossom and bear fruit, signaling a promising harvest. Of particular importance to crops in this period is water, and farmers work hard to protect against drought.

Chushu (Limit of Heat)

In Chinese, *chu* means disposal and *chushu* implies that the summer heat will soon disappear. *Chushu* occurs on the 23rd or 24th of August. After *chushu*, most parts of China see a gradual reduction in precipitation and a wider temperature gap between the night and the day. A warm day plus a cool night is highly beneficial for crop nutrition. Cold air has a good chance of moving southward at *chushu*. However, due to the effects of global warming, southern China still experiences a high temperature reaching around 35 degrees Celsius. However, the hot weather does not last long as the worst heat is over.

Bailu (White Dew)

A popular saying advises "Do not go naked at bailu"; it is no longer proper to be stripped to the waist at *bailu* due to the cool weather.

Lu refers to dew. Due to low temperatures at night, vapor condenses into water droplets. *Bailu* falls on the 7th or 8th of September when the weather turns really cool. In most parts of China, the sky is clear and high and the weather agreeable and serene at this time.

Cotton is bursting into white wool.

The golden fields stretch as far as the eye can see.

Bailu signals the arrival of the harvest season, when fields turn into a vast stretch of golden yellow. It is time to gather in grain crops, soy beans, and sorghum grown on the plains of northern China, while cotton bursts into white wool on either side of the Yangtze River. *Bailu* is also a planting season, and winter wheat is planted in the northwest and northeast of China. *Bailu* therefore signals a hectic, tough, but joyful season.

Bailu represents typical dry autumn weather. To deal with dry weather condition, it is advisable to eat more fruit and foods which are full of vitamins.

Qiufen (The Autumnal Equinox)

The autumnal equinox and the vernal equinox have something in common: the night and the day are almost of equal length. The only difference is that after the vernal equinox the days gradually get longer and the nights shorter while with autumnal equinox it is the other way round.

After the autumnal equinox, cold air currents move southward and run headlong into warm air currents, with the effect that precipitation keeps occurring and temperatures drop. As a result, the weather gradually becomes cooler.

Hanlu (Cold Dew)

An old saying advises "Do not expose your feet at *hanlu*" as, to avoid getting sick, it is no longer suitable to go barefoot due to cool weather. After *hanlu*, it is cool both in the morning and in the evening. As the weather is unpredictable, those in poor health need to take care to keep themselves warm.

Hanlu occurs in early October when dew is colder than at *bailu*. In the northeast and northwest of China, winter is round the corner and in Beijing and its vicinity, early frost begins to appear. In most parts of China the rainy season is already over by this time.

Shuangjiang (The Descent of Frost)

Taking the term at its face value, *shuangjiang* suggests cold weather. *Shuangjiang* occurs in late October. Frost occurring for the first time in autumn is generally referred to as "early frost" or "initial frost", while frost occurring for the last time in spring is referred to as "late frost" or "terminal frost". The earlier the frost season sets in, the more damage is caused to farming. Nationwide, frost makes an earlier appearance in the north than in the south.

In some areas, frost-bite occurs at *shuangjiang*. Caused by a drastic decrease in temperature, frost inflicts damage on crops, the extent of which varies according to the breed and stage of development of the individual crop.

Scientifically speaking, frost and frost-bite are two different concepts. Frost-biting can occur in the absence of frost, and vice versa.

Lidong (The Start of Winter)

Lidong falls on the 7th or 8th of November. The connotations of most seasonal division points are easily identifiable from their names. This is also the case with *lidong*, which signifies the arrival of winter. *Li* means to establish or start. *Lidong* represents the start of another season, as is the case with *lichun*, *lixia* and *liqiu*.

After *lidong*, heat radiation from the sun gradually decreases throughout the northern hemisphere, which causes a corresponding reduction in heat conservation on the surface of the earth and a further drop in temperature. In this period, leaves wither and turn yellow, migrating birds fly south, and insects crawl into holes. Meanwhile, many animals prepare for hibernation. Natural disasters such as gusts of wind and cold spells need occur during this time.

In China, people are in the habit of giving their health a boost in winter through certain foods or herbal tonics. Human beings do not hibernate, but in severely cold weather the metabolism slows down, meaning that whatever is taken for health improvement is more easily absorbed into the body. According to traditional Chinese medicine, energy and life lie dormant in the winter. The *yang* force inherent in the human body is stored up while nature transforms. Winter diets should therefore focus on high-calorie foods in addition to vegetables and vitamin supplements.

Xiaoxue (Minor Snow)

Xiaoxue period starts on the 22nd or 23rd of November and ends on the 7th or 8th of December. During this period, cold spells and severely cold air currents are highly active. Frost has already descended in the northeast and northwest of China, which signifies that winter has appeared in all these regions. Winter is also making its way to the middle and lower reaches of the Yangtze River. As a result of a significant drop in temperature, precipitation occurs, but more in the areas south of the Yangtze River than in the north. The weather therefore becomes cold and damp, which makes it hard for northerners to acclimatize if they happen to be on a visit in the south.

The damp, chilly, and bleak weather at *xiaoxue* tends to cause emotional imbalance. This can be offset by increased exercise, outdoor activities, and basking in any available sunshine.

Daxue (Major Snow)

Following in the wake of *xiaoxue*, *daxue* falls on the 7th or 8th of December, which suggests even colder weather on the way and possibly even snow.

A well-known Chinese saying notes that "Heavy snow promises a

Winter snow promises a bumper crop.

bumper crop". When covered with snow, the crops and the ground can maintain a well-controlled temperature, safe from cold spells. Snow also moistens crops and so keeps them safe from drought. Furthermore, snow is known to kill many pests.

It goes without saying that snow also brings about disasters. Heavy snowstorms are the biggest threat to agricultural production. In addition, excessive snow poses a severe road hazard.

In this period, the temperature drops to 10 degrees below zero in the northeast and northwest of China, zero degree and below in the Yellow River and northern areas, and about 5 degrees in the south.

Dongzhi (The Winter Solstice)

Dongzhi occurs in late December. It is mentioned above that *dongzhi* marks the shortest day but the longest night of the year in the northern hemisphere. The reason for this is that the sun casts its light almost vertically on the Tropic of Capricorn. As a result, the southern hemisphere is in full summer, while the northern hemisphere is exposed to sunlight for only a limited period of time. In fact, the further north one travels, the less daylight there is. At the North Pole, the sun is still invisible even at midday. After *dongzhi*, daylight gradually migrates northward, as a result of which the days grow longer in the northern hemisphere. At *dongzhi*, more heat is absorbed than dissipated on the surface of the earth. People in China normally start counting in nines after *dongzhi*, because a saying tells them to "Count by the nine to figure out the coldest days". This means that nine days can be counted as one unit, and when the calculation reaches the third unit (roughly 25 days after *dongzhi*), the coldest period of the year sets in.

The Chinese treat *dongzhi* as a holiday. It is said that celebrations of *dongzhi* originated in the Han Dynasty, attained prominence during the Tang and Song Dynasties, and have persisted to this day. In the past, people believed that the *yin* and *yang* forces could transform themselves into each other on this day, and it was consequently a good day to receive blessings from Heaven. During the Tang and Song Dynasties, emperors made a point of making excursions to the outskirts of cities to conduct grand sacrificial ceremonies, while common people paid their respect to their parents and the elderly. Celebration is carried on to this day by slaughtering pigs and sheep and eating *jiaozi* in the north of China, and by eating *dongzhi* rice balls and longevity noodles in the south. These practices, though rare in big cities, is relatively common in rural areas.

Xiaohan (Minor Cold)

Xiaohan occurs on the 5th or 6th day of the first month of the Western calendar. The coldest days usually descend sometime between *xiaohan* and *dahan*. It is in this period that the "third nine" mentioned above occurs. A popular saying states that "*Xiaohan* out-colds *dahan*," which means that it is colder in the former period than in the latter. By this time, the heat stored in the surface of the earth has been totally released. While little heat is absorbed during the day, a good deal of it is released at night, which is a situation of "income falling short of expenditure". Meteorological data compiled in various parts of China all point to the fact that the coldest weather occurs during the *xiaohan* period.

Dahan (Major Cold)

Dahan is the last of the twenty-four seasonal division points and occurs around the 20th of January. Although the character *da* denotes the severity of cold weather, *dahan* in fact suggests anything but the coldest weather, as discussed above. There are exceptions, however. In certain years and in certain coastal areas, the lowest temperature of the year can occur during this period. At *dahan*, it is necessary to continue to take preventive measures to protect crops and cattle.

As *dahan* comes right before *lichun*, with the Spring Festival just around the corner, a festive atmosphere fills the air. At this juncture, people always find themselves busily occupied in writing summary reports, looking back over the past year's work, looking forward to the future, and mapping out new goals. It is common to see smiling people walking through the streets carrying bags meant for the Spring Festival celebration. It is no wonder that this period is referred to as the holiday season throughout the world.

Culinary Delights of China

China boasts a unique and rich culinary culture. The same food can be made into various kinds of dishes. For instance, bamboo shoots can be utilized in many different ways to create a feast of hundreds of diverse bamboo shoot dishes. Think also of the many unique dishes that all use chicken as the central ingredient. Over time, the Chinese have developed cookery into an art form.

Different provinces have different flavor preferences and use different techniques in the preparation of meals, thus creating a surprisingly diverse range of local culinary delights. The following are a few "picks" from different areas.

Shanghai Steamed Juicy Dumplings (*Xiao Long Bao*)

Xiao Long Bao are a well-known snack from Shanghai, and those made in Nanxiang Town, located in Shanghai's Jiading District, are particularly renowned. To make the small and exquisite *Xiao Long Bao*, first cut the well-kneaded dough into small pieces, which should be

Xiao Long Bao (Shanghai Steamed Juicy Dumplings)

flattened into thin flat circles. Next, add the meat filling and fold the dough over the filling toward the center to seal the dumpling, and then put into a steamer. *Xiao Long Bao* may be easy to make, but there are very special requirements concerning the dough and the filling. Though the dough does not need to be leavened, the water added into the flour and the kneading must be carried out particularly carefully to ensure that the dumplings appear thin and translucent after having been steamed. The filling has to be even more stringently prepared to make sure that it remains soft and retains its tasty juices.

There is also a unique ritual involved in the eating of *Xiao Long Bao*. If you are not careful, the juices may leak out, which will not only spoil the taste, but will also ruin your clothes. As *Xiao Long Bao* are served steaming hot, you are advised to first pick one up carefully with chopsticks and place it on a spoon, then bite a small hole in the outer coating and slowly sip the juices. It should be eaten while steaming hot, so be careful not to burn your tongue.

Spring rolls are being fried.

Besides those in Nanxiang Town, reputed *Xiao Long Bao* restaurants can also be found in the City God Temple in downtown Shanghai.

Spring Rolls

Spring rolls are fried pastries from the south of China, with those from Shanghai and Guangdong being the best known.

The name is intrinsically linked to the Spring Festival. In the past, the Chinese had the custom of having "spring pancakes" to mark the end of winter. These "spring pancakes" are actually rolled pancakes with different fillings. By the Yuan Dynasty, fried spring pancakes, an early form of spring rolls, had appeared.

Spring rolls are common in south China and can be found not only during the Spring Festival, but also in restaurants at any time of the year. Many people also make spring rolls at home.

Spring rolls are relatively easy to make. Mix flour with a small amount of water and knead into a very soft paste. Spread out the paste to make round and paper-thin sheets on a heated griddle. Cool these sheets, add a filling, and then wrap them into long rolls. Deep-fry the rolls until golden. In cities, spring roll sheets can be bought in stores, making the job easier.

The filling can be either sweet or savory depending on your preference. For a sweet filling, sweetened bean paste is a good choice. For a savory one, Chinese cabbage and shredded pork is particularly popular, while shredded bamboo shoots and edible fungus can be added for good measure. The filling should be thickened with cornstarch and left to cool before use, as hot fillings tend to break the outer casing. The skins of perfect spring rolls should be crispy, and the filling tender.

Pita Bread Soaked in Mutton Soup (*Yang Rou Pao Mo*)

The capital of China for six dynasties, Xi'an is an ancient city full of history and culture. It is also famous for its wonderful snacks and local delicacies, of which *Yang Rou Pao Mo* is a good example.

Known as "Thick Mutton Soup" in ancient times, *Yang Rou Pao Mo* is

actually broken bread soaked in mutton soup.

Though it sounds simple, the preparation can be incredibly complex. There are particular steps which must be followed when brewing the soup and baking the bread.

Yang Rou Pao Mo (Pita bread soaked in Mutton Soup)

To make good soup, it is important to choose good quality mutton. The meat should be washed and then soaked for about half an hour, after which the blood should be skimmed from the surface. Next, place the washed mutton in a wok, add water and seasoning, such as Chinese prickly ash, star anise, fennel, cassia bark, spring onions and ginger, and stew until the meat has appeared to melt into the thick broth.

Pita bread is more popular than pancakes in Xi'an, owing to the historical influence of the sizeable Muslim community. To make pita bread, the dough must be well-kneaded before being put aside for half an hour. Pieces of dough should then be flattened into small pies and baked without oil over a low heat. They should be served just before they are fully cooked.

Yang Rou Pao Mo is served in a distinctive way. Coriander and bean vermicelli may be added to the soup according to preference, before the bread is broken into small pieces and dipped in the soup. When the bread is fully soaked, it is ready. Tasty soup and chewy bread make up the uniquely flavored *Yang Rou Pao Mo*. In the north of China, chili sauce and sweetened garlic are often added for variety.

Old Sun's House and Tong Sheng Xiang are the most famous among the many *Yang Rou Pao Mo* establishments in Xi'an.

Beijing Roast Duck

Beijing Roast Duck, traditionally known in the West as Peking Duck, is prepared using a special variety of duck raised in Beijing. According to a local story, during the Ming Dynasty the emperor ordered that a canal be dredged to allow the transport of high quality grains from the southern bank of the Yangtze River to Beijing. A tremendous amount of manpower was deployed, and the canal was constructed in no time. Barges carrying the imperial grains were soon on their way to the northern capital along the canal. However, due to poor supervision, grains often fell into the river, and so the ducks that lived along the canal

Chefs are preparing Beijing Roast duck.

around the capital began to feed on them. Gradually, the ducks grew fat and their meat became more tender and tasty. Later, a special variety of ducks with succulent and tender meat, a bigger body and a thin skin were raised in Beijing, and became an instant hit with local diners.

Beijing ducks are typically white-feathered, stout with long and wide bodies and thick and short legs. Their beaks are short and wide, with a colour somewhere between orange and yellow. Beijing Roast Ducks are known for their crisp skin, succulent and tender meat, and brilliant color.

The most famous restaurant which serves this specialty is Quanjude in Beijing. Quanjude is renowned throughout the country for producing the best roast ducks. Quangjude roasts its ducks by hanging the birds on a rack in an oven, directly over the burning wood of peach, jujube or date trees. Through the glass windows of Quanjude restaurants in Beijing, one can see a mouth-watering display of gleaming Beijing roast ducks over the ovens. It takes about 45 minutes to roast a duck. On leaving the oven, the duck should be a deep dark red, with crisp skin and tender meat and a pleasant aroma of wood and fruits.

Roast duck should be sliced into thin pieces and rolled into lotus leaf-shaped pancakes. This is because the duck is too rich to be consumed in large amounts on its own. Furthermore, since no seasoning is added during the roasting, sauces are needed to heighten the flavor of the finished dish.

There are three major sauces that may accompany the roast duck: sweet bean sauce with thin lengths of scallion, to go with cucumber and radish slices; soybean sauce with mashed garlic, to go with pieces of radish; and powdered sugar. The sweet bean sauce is the most popular of the three. A small amount of the sauce is spread on the palm-sized lotus leaf-shaped pancakes, before the meat, cucumber and scallion are added, and then it is rolled up into a thin envelope.

The quality of the duck varies with the seasons, and the best times to enjoy it are spring, autumn and winter. Summer is a less popular time to eat roast duck, because the heat puts people off greasy food and Beijing ducks tend to lose weight in summer, compromising the taste of the roast.

Quanjude was founded in 1864 (the third year of Emperor Tongzhi's reign during the Qing Dynasty). After over a century of development and innovation, Quanjude has developed menus for duck feasts, and offers more than 400 dishes on its menu. It has now become a well-known name around the world, impressing peoples of different countries with its delicious delicacies.

Instant-boiled Mutton (*Shuan Yang Rou*)

Another Beijing specialty, *Shuan Yang Rou* is very easy to prepare, and you do not have to be a professional chef to be able to master it. Donglaishun and Zhengyanglou make the best *Shuan Yang Rou* in Beijing.

To prepare this dish, remove the skin and bone of a leg of lamb, and slice it into pieces of around 12 centimeters long and 2 centimeters wide. Other ingredients that can go with the meat include cellophane noodles and spinach, among other vegetables. After the noodles are softened in hot water and the spinach is rinsed, place them on plates. Arrange the lamb slices on a separate platter.

The taste of the dish has a lot to do with the dipping sauce, as a good sauce should enhance the flavor. Ingredients for the sauce usually include soy sauce, shrimp concentrate, sesame jam, chili oil, fermented tofu juice, and leek, which are used in various combinations according to the preferences of the diner.

To make this dish, first put some water in the pot and add chicken stock or pork stock. Traditional hot pots are heated with charcoal, but modern ones usually use gas or electricity. Gas is preferred by restaurants, while electrical hot pots are more common at home. When the stock is brought to a boil, use your chopsticks to add the

Donglaishun, an old restaurant in Beijing, is famous for its *Shuan Yang Rou* (instant-boiled Mutton).

An exquisite hot pot

slices of lamb, and cook for one or two minutes. When the meat turns gray, dip it in the accompanying sauce and enjoy. Cook one helping at a time, and remove from the stock once cooked, to ensure that the meat remains tender. Spinach and cellophane noodles are usually added to the stock after the lamb is finished. By then the stock will be suffused with flavor.

There are many stories about the origin of *Shuan Yang Rou*. The most popular involves Kublai Khan, an emperor of the Yuan Dynasty. Roughly a thousand years ago, Kublai Khan led his army on an expedition to conquer the Southern Song. After a long day of travel, the army were both hungry and tired. Suddenly, Kublai Khan thought of a dish in his hometown—steamed mutton. He ordered his men to make it for him. Just as the chef was busy slaughtering the sheep, a sentinel reported that enemies were coming. However, the chef did not want to deprive his leader of his dinner. He then struck upon an idea: he quickly

Business in restaurants specializing in hot pots is booming in winter.

sliced the mutton, boiled it in hot water, added some salt and seasoning, and presented it to Kublai Khan, who finished his meal before riding off to fight his enemies. After the battle was won, Kublai Khan specifically ordered the dish in celebration. After feeding the delighted army, the chef took the chance to ask Kublai Khan to give the dish a name. Kublai Khan said with a smile: "Let us call it instant-boiled mutton!"

Hot Pot

Hot pot is similar to instant-boiled mutton, except that the term covers a wider range of recipes. You can put in any meat or vegetable of your choice. As a result, there are a wide variety of hot pots, such as Sichuan spicy hot pot, light hot pot from the South and exquisite Taiwan-style hot pot.

Sichuan hot pot is the best-known. Whether using a spicy red stock or a plain white stock, Sichuan people always manage to produce strong and rich hot pots, making sure that you will never forget it. For meat-lovers, the ingredients can include goose guts, duck guts, beef, tripe, fish heads and different kinds of game; for vegetarians, different varieties of mushrooms are available, such as golden needle mushroom or enoki

Making *nang*

mushroom, Queen Bolete, oyster mushroom, as well as all kinds of edible fungus and matsutake. Green vegetables are also very popular choices.

The stock is the key to a good hot pot. The taste of hot pot varies from restaurant to restaurant, as each one will have its own recipe. Most common are chicken stock, pork rib stock, and seafood stock seasoned with a number of spices and flavorings. Restaurants usually consider their stock recipes trade secrets.

The pots themselves are traditionally made of copper and heated with charcoal. As charcoal pollutes the environment and copper rust is harmful to health, copper pots are now almost extinct, and have been replaced with electrical stainless steel pots, which have the added benefit of adjustable heat.

As it is rich in fat and high in calories, as well as often being very spicy, hot pot is most popular in winter. When cooking meat in a hot pot, you must pay special attention to the heat, as it causes the loss of tenderness and nutrition if overcooked, and digestive problems if undercooked. Food leaving the pot is very hot, so wait for it to cool before you sample it. Moderation must be practiced for this delight, because your glands will be overtaxed by the need to produce gastric juice and bile non-stop to cope with the prolonged exposure to hot food, causing gastro-enteric dysfunctions such as diarrhea and stomach-ache. Also, hot pot contains a high level of purine, bad for people suffering from gout.

Uighur-style Crusty Pancake (*Nang*)

As the main staple food of local Uighurs and Kazaks in western Xinjiang, the wheat pancakes there are said to have been eaten for more than two thousand years.

There are different varieties of *nang*, such as *rou nang* (with meat), *you nang* (with suet), sesame *nang* and *pian nang* (wheel-sized). *Nang* is prepared in a similar way to pancakes. Water and baking powder are mixed with flour and a pinch of salt, and is kneaded before being set aside to rise. The ingredients and baking methods are reflected in the names; hence, pancakes with suet become *you nang*, and those with diced meat, cumin powder and pepper are called *rou nang*.

These crusty pancakes must be made in a special oven. Built of mud and mixed with loess, wheat straws and human hair, or bricks, it can be square or round, but the inner pit must be hollow and

Freshly-baked nice-smelling *nangs*

tapered. To bake the *nang*, burning coal or charcoal is put in the pit, and, once the smoke is gone and the pit wall is fully heated, *nang* is lined on the wall to bake. In Xinjiang, a baking oven can be found in most village houses, and many in cities. Baked *nang* is thin and crisp in the middle, and thick and puffy around the edge. The sizes range between 50 and 20 centimeters in diameter. During festivals, locals celebrate by building pagodas of different-sized *nang*.

Nang is dry and can be kept for a long time, and is thus often taken on long journeys. This also explains why many ethnic groups in Xinjiang have been eating *nang* for such a long time. When they were nomadic, they were often on long treks, and so the easy-to-carry and durable *nang* became their best choice for food. It is said that dried *nang* is even a lenitive for diseases, such as gastritis.

There is a famous *nang* street in Yining City, Xinjiang, which is home to over 60 *nang* restaurants. Many ethnic groups have *nang* for breakfast, with some even eating it with all three meals in a day, thus providing the street with a constant stream of business.

Two *La Mian* masters are hand-stretching noodles.

Hand-stretched Noodles (*La Mian*)

La Mian are a well-known traditional specialty of Shanxi. *La Mian*-making has become a popular show that can be seen on almost every street in Shanxi. The most intriguing part is that when a slab of dough is stretched into countless slim coils of noodles; in the hands of a *La Mian* master, it can remain as a single amazingly long noodle.

Making *La Mian* requires a lot of finesse. Different types of La Mian call for different levels of accomplishment. *Da La Mian* (big stretched noodles) are usually of less than seven coils. Those with more than seven coils are called Dragon Whisker Noodles, and tend to be fine and slim. *Xiao La Mian* (little stretched noodles), with more than seven coils, tend to be the ones most often cooked by families at home.

There are four steps in making *La Mian*: making the dough, shaking the dough, stretching the noodles, and finally cooking. When making the dough, mix, 50 grams of water,1 gram of salt and a small amount of baking soda with every 100 grams of flour. After mixing, put aside for about twenty minutes, and then knead into a slab. The next part is perhaps the most important: hold the two ends of the dough, shake and stretch it repeatedly to make it even, then place it on a chopping board and fold it in two. After repeating the process several times, you will see the dough transformed into slim strips of noodles. When well-stretched, put them down on the board and sprinkle with dry flour: they are now ready for cooking. *La Mian* should be soft and smooth, yet slightly chewy.

Of the different kinds of *La Mian*, Dragon Whisker Noodles certainly have the most distinguished pedigree. They originated in the imperial court and later became popular among the common people. A *La Mian* master can stretch a slab of dough into noodles as fine as a single hair. In Shanxi, Dragon Whisker Noodles, a symbol of longevity and happiness, are a must-have at birthday dinners and family gatherings.

Sliced Noodles (*Dao Xiao Mian*)

Dao Xiao Mian is also a well-known noodle dish from Shanxi. In noodle shops in Shanxi, it is common to see the chef holding a lump of dough up to the shoulder with one hand, with a knife in the other, and proceed to peel thin slices of noodles rapidly off the surface of the dough, letting them fall into a pot of boiling water in front of him. This is exactly how *Dao Xiao Mian* should be made. Thick in the middle and thin around the edges, these sliced noodles are shaped like willow leaves, smooth and chewy, soft and dry.

Dao Xiao Mian are said to have been created during the Qin Dynasty.

After unifying China, the Emperor ordered that all weapons in the country be confiscated in order to prevent rebellions. This included kitchen knives. One day, when a man was making noodles, a staple food in northwestern China, he found a piece of iron on the ground. After cleaning it, he found that it could be used to slice the dough into thin pieces which could then be cooked. Others soon followed suit and *Dao Xiao Mian* were born.

As the name implies, *Dao Xiao Mian* are sliced with knives, which are specifically made for that purpose. The knife is an arc-shaped razor, which ensures that the noodle slices are thick in the middle and thin at the edges.

The ratio of flour to water must be exactly right when making *Dao Xiao Mian*: too much water makes the dough mushy, and means that it will stick to the blade; too little water hardens the dough, and means that it will easily break. A master can make between 180 and 200 slices in a minute, all twenty centimeters long. Like *La Mian* masters, a *Dao Xiao Mian* master must be graceful in his movements, which should resemble those of a skilled violinist playing his instrument.

Beijing Noodles with Spicy Meat Sauce
(*Zha Jiang Mian*)

A special feature of Beijing, *Zha Jiang Mian* are cooked noodles topped with a special sauce which determines the taste of the dish.

Good quality spicy sauces are not easy to make. Take the most common diced pork sauce, for example. Diced pork must first be sautéd with scallion, ginger and garlic, before bean paste is added, and the dish is then covered and left to simmer down. Water is added, and when the sauce turns lustrously dark it is ready. Bean sauce produced by the century-old Liu Bi Ju Pickles Store is the best of its kind and very popular with Beijing natives. There are a variety of sauces that can be used in making *Zha Jiang Mian*. Besides diced pork sauce, there is the Three

Zha Jiang Mian (noodles with spicy meat sauce)

Delicacies Sauce (including shrimp, pork loin and winter bamboo shoots), egg sauce, diced tofu sauce, braised eggplant mince sauce and many others.

Buddha Jumps over the Wall (*Fo Tiao Qiang*)

One of the top local dishes in Fujian, *Fo Tiao Qiang* is also very popular in Guangdong and Hong Kong. Made with seafood, poultry and different types of red meat, it is known for its high nutritional value and exquisite taste.

It is said that the dish originated in the Qing Dynasty. At that time, the ingredients only included various seafood, chicken, duck, the upper part of mutton leg and pigeon's egg. Now, through generations of improvement, the soup is more delicious than ever.

Prepared with more than 20 ingredients, including shark's fin, ham, sea cucumber, winter bamboo shoots, fish lips, fish maw, pork tendon, abalone, chicken, mushroom, duck gizzard and lotus leaf, and stewed over a low fire

The dish *Fo Tiao Qiang* (literally "Buddha jumping over the wall")

in a wine jar, it is rich and aromatic, and will literally melt in your mouth.

Rice Noodle Rolls (*Chang Fen*)

Chang Fen are a Cantonese snack made of rice. To make *Chang Fen*, put rice pulp in custom-made multi-layer steamers, where it should remain until it has hardened into thin sheets. After taking out the sheets, put in meat fillets, slices of fish or shrimp, roll them into long strips and steam once again.

The perfect *Chang Fen* are as white as snow and as thin as sheets of paper, while remaining glutinous and smooth. Different types of rice noodle rolls have different fillings, such as beef, pork, fish and shrimp. Rolls can be made without any filling, and sweet rolls can be made from rice pulp laced with sugar.

Chang Fen are one of the popular snacks in south China, and are usually washed down with tea, particularly in tea houses, restaurants and snack bars in Guangdong and Hong Kong.

Appetizing *Chang Fen* (rice noodle rolls).

Cross-Bridge Rice Noodles
(*Guo Qiao Mi Xian*)

Rice Noodles (*Mi Xian*) are also called rice vermicelli (*Mi Fen*) in Guangdong, and fine noodles (*Xian Fen*) in Guangxi. Unique to Yunnan, Cross-Bridge Rice Noodles were created more than 100 years ago and have become famous for the special way in which they are served. According to folklore, a young scholar retreated to a small island to focus on his preparations for the imperial examination. His wife would bring him his meals every day. However, as their home was a long way from the island, his meals would often have become cold by the time they reached him. One day, his wife brought him some chicken soup and his favorite rice noodles. When she was removing it from the hamper, her fingers got burnt by the soup bowl: it had stayed hot because of a layer of oil on the top. She then added the rice noodles to the soup. Her husband was impressed that the meal tasted as if it was freshly cooked. To show his appreciation, her husband named the dish "Cross-Bridge Rice Noodles" after the fact that his wife had to cross a bridge to reach the small island. The dish has since become very popular.

"Cross-Bridge" also refers to the way the dish is prepared: the rice noodles and other ingredients are first placed in small dishes adjacent to the soup, and there is later a process of transition or "bridge-crossing". When it is served, you will be presented with a selection of raw ingredients and rice noodles, and then a big pot of hot soup. All you have to do is empty the ingredients and the rice noodles into the soup, wait a few minutes, and then enjoy the dish. When you put in the ingredients, be careful that you put the

Guo Qiao Mi Xian, a Yunan specialty

meat when the soup is still boiling, and add the vegetables later, as it takes longer for the meat to cook. The rice noodles should be added at the end.

The soup is a special kind of broth made from chicken or pork bones. The thick layer of oil on the surface of the soup helps keep the soup hot enough to cook the other ingredients. The ingredients that are traditionally added to the dish include thin slices of pork loin, fish, leek, sheets of tofu and bean sprouts.

Rice noodles are made from ground rice, and look like ordinary noodles. There are two types of rice noodles in Yunnan. One type is made from fermented rice and called fermented rice noodles. Fermented rice noodles are complex to make, and should be chewy, smooth and aromatic. The other type is called dry pulp rice noodles, as they are machine-pressed from ground rice. After being machine- or sun-dried, the noodles are a convenient shape and size for storage and transportation. These rice noodles need to be steamed to allow them to expand before cooking.

Folk dancers are performing at a Chinese New Year fair in Beijing.

Indigenous Customs

Chinese civilization is one of the oldest in the world. In the past, natural phenomena that could not be explained were often attributed to divine actions and so, in order to understand the relationship between the supernatural world and visible events, a number of customs came into being. These customs and superstitions commonly express people's yearning and desire for a happy and prosperous life and became a way of meeting the spiritual needs of the populace.

Since China is a vast country containing many ethnic groups, there are a number of distinct indigenous customs. However, many of these traditional indigenous customs are interrelated, interdependent, and interlocked, and have survived to this day.

Posting "Happiness" Upside Down

At the Spring Festival, it is common practice to paste the character for "Happiness" on the doors, windows and walls of every household. However, the character is often pasted upside down.

Zhu Yuanzhang, a Ming Dynasty emperor, once used the character for

A giant character "Happiness" is hanging in a shopping mall.

"Happiness" as a secret mark which distinguished which of his opponents he wanted killed. In order to abort the bloodshed, Empress Ma ordered that the character for "Happiness" be posted on the gate of every household in the city. However, one illiterate family posted the character upside down. The next day, Emperor Zhu Yuanzhang burst into a fit of rage when he found out what had happened, and decided to single out the illiterate family for capital punishment to vent his anger. Empress Ma, sensing that the situation had got out of hand, said to the Emperor, "That family purposely posted the character upside down in order to welcome your arrival, which is the arrival of happiness. Don't you see the meaning of all of this?" [In Chinese, "upside down" has the same pronunciation as "arrival".] The Emperor decided that the Empress' words made sense and acquitted the illiterate family. Since then, the character for "Happiness" has been posted upside down to signal the arrival of happiness and good fortune.

Red Eggs

In China, the birth of a baby is an occasion for celebration. It is common practice throughout the country to give eggs dyed with red rice to relatives and friends as a sign of celebration.

Some argue that the custom of dyeing eggs originated in ancient cultures which invested particular importance on fertility. On the other hand, the color red is synonymous with good fortune and prosperity in China. That explains why eggs that are dyed red have been used to celebrate the birth of a new life and the survival of the family name.

In ancient societies, the chicken was worshipped as the king of all animals for its alleged ability to subjugate devils and monsters. And eggs produced by it and in turn produced chickens were looked upon as sacred. It was also once believed that devils and monsters could only be thwarted by sacred eggs.

The "Snatching" Ritual

The "snatching" ritual occurs on the one-month anniversary of a baby's birth. Before birthday noodles are served at noon, a large table piled with different objects (such as seals, books, paper and pens, an abacus, tidbits, and toys, plus cooking utensils and needles and thread in the case of a baby girl) is placed by the side of a bed. The baby is then encouraged to snatch an object without guidance in order to establish the child's character and possible future. The snatching of books, for instance, is interpreted as showing that the child may become a scholar; the snatching of a seal shows that the child may become an official; while the snatching of an abacus shows that the child may become a businessman.

The "snatching" ritual reflects the high hopes parents have for their children, as well as their desire to bestow blessings. In modern society, what is snatched by the baby is no longer important, and the outcome of the ritual is not usually taken too seriously.

Visiting a Daughter's Former Home

A married daughter is supposed to visit her former home on certain days, accompanied by her husband and children, to pay respects to her parents. Such a visit occurs on the second or the third day of the first lunar month in most parts of China. The reason for this is that departed ancestors, according to superstition, return home to receive sacrifices at the end of the lunar year, but will not enter if an outsider is present, and a married daughter is looked upon as an outsider. Therefore, a married daughter is barred from appearing at her former home on Spring Festival Eve and New Year's Day.

This ancient rule, although now ignored in big cities, are still followed with rigor in rural areas, where violation of this custom would be frowned upon.

Birthday Noodles

Birthday noodles are as common in China as birthday cakes are in Western countries. During the Tang Dynasty a custom originated of celebrating the birth of a baby boy with cake soup, which was the predecessor of noodle soup. Long noodles suggest longevity. Since they are often served at birthday parties, they are known as "birthday noodles".

She Huo

She huo refers to the various acrobatic stunts and variety shows

Chinese local residents perform folk art in Qinghai province.

seen in the past as a way to offer sacrifice to the God of Land and the God of Fire. *She* refers to the God of Land, and *huo* to the God of Fire. Since ancient China was an agrarian country, the influence of these two gods was deep-seated, and offering sacrifice to them was a common occurrence.

With the passage of time, *she huo* has lost its sacrificial element, but still retains its recreational aspects. *She huo* is very popular in northern Shanxi and involves roughly 200 different activities, such as folk dancing, the playing of gongs and drums, and the performance of martial arts. These exciting and entertaining performances are thought to bring good luck, happiness, and physical and mental well-being to both the participants and the viewers.

Chinese Talismans

Objects often provide a window to a person's character and feelings, and may be used to express certain sentiments and aspirations. The Chinese endow objects, both imaginary and real, with auspicious meanings to express their ideas and feelings. The kylin and the dragon, for instance, are sacred creatures in the eyes of the Chinese, and they occupy a special place in traditional Chinese culture. Images of the kylin and the dragon can be found in paintings, clothing and embroidery, and are thought to bring spiritual gratification.

The Chinese invest a lot of importance in talismans which they believe aid them throughout their daily life and provide spiritual comfort.

The Kylin

The kylin is a sacred mythological animal that appears in ancient legends. The kylin, the phoenix, the turtle and the dragon are collectively known as the "four sacred animals".

The kylin body is thought to resemble a deer's, while it is said to have an ox's tail, a horse's hooves, and to be covered with fish-like

Bronze kylins are guarding the Palace Museum.

scales. The four animals which the kylin resembles are all believed to bring good luck and happiness. The collection and intermingling of these positive aspects is a typical feature of the Chinese imagination.

Legend has it that the kylin is mild and non-confrontational, since it is thought to embody the ideals of Confucianism. It is also considered to be a "Benevolent Animal", which can bring happiness, enhance fertility, and uphold justice. It is therefore extremely popular. Its likeness can be found in traditional Chinese painting, embroidery, architecture, and sculpture, where it is used to signify good luck and a bright future.

The Dragon

The dragon is said to have a deer's horn, an ox's head, a serpent's body, a fish's scales and an eagle's claws. The dragon is portrayed as awe-inspiring, fearless and omnipotent, a symbol of power and authority. It is little wonder that in ancient China, the emperor was regarded as the

Nine Dragon Wall in Beihai Park in Beijing in winter

reincarnation of the dragon.

China's fondness for the dragon began in the early stage of the Neolithic period, grew throughout the Shang and Zhou Dynasties, and developed mass popular appeal during the Qin and Han Dynasties. The image of the Chinese dragon, used for more than a thousand years, is inextricably linked to the development of Chinese culture. According to ancient Chinese mythology, the dragon created the earth, participated in the development of humankind, and assisted Yu the Great, founder of the Xia Dynasty, in harnessing the rivers. Furthermore, Chinese people consider themselves to be "the Dragon's Descendents".

For thousands of years, the concept of the dragon has permeated every sphere of Chinese life. The dragon is therefore the symbol of China as a nation and of Chinese culture. In the eyes of the Chinese people, the

A two-hundred-year-old sea turtle at the sea world in Tianjin Aquarium Museum is seen wearing a garment with the character "Longevity."

dragon is sacred, and the signifies the spirit of unity, endeavor, innovation, and creation.

The Phoenix

In feudal societies, the phoenix was regarded as a sacred bird and worshipped as the God of Protection. It is characterized by a golden pheasant's head, a mandarin duck's body, an eagle's wings, a crane's legs, a parrot's beak and a peacock's tail. Its beauty means that it is always closely associated with the feminine, and is thought of as the counterpart of the dragon (which symbolizes the emperor).

The Turtle

Unlike the dragon and the phoenix, turtles exist outside myths and legends. The turtle is regarded as a lucky talisman because of its long life span, and is therefore synonymous with longevity.

Chinese Knots

With only a few simple movements, a single length of string can be made to create a beautiful pattern with a symmetrical left and right,

Chinese knots are on display.

an identical back and front, and the top and bottom ends left ready for coupling. This simplicity is part of the beauty of Chinese knot-tying.

Before the creation of a written language, the Chinese used knots as a way of recording events. The tying of different knots later emerged as a decorative art during the Tang Dynasty, and was invested with symbolic meaning during successive dynasties. For example, a "long twisted knot" signifies everlasting love and devotion, a "golden money knot" means wealth will be forthcoming, and a "longevity knot" is worn around a child's neck in the hope of promoting a long life. Meanwhile, "double fish knots", "bat knots" and "butterfly knots" are all thought to help change life for the better. Chinese knots come in a wide variety.

Although Chinese knot-tying has lost its practical function, it is still widely enjoyed, and is now considered to be an art in its own right.

Chinese knot-tying involves coiling, sliding, twining, winding, weaving and pulling, always using only one single length of cord. The typical cord used for Chinese knot-tying is 100 cm long and 4 - 6 mm in diameter, with colored silk threads twirled into the cord. The advantage of using silk thread is its bright color and luster.

Recent years have witnessed a revival in traditional Chinese folk art and craft, and Chinese knot-tying is becoming particularly popular. At many festivals, there is often a huge selection of Chinese knots for sale. As well as large tapestries and wall hangings, more contemporary knotted decorations have emerged, such as wrist chains, necklaces, sashes and rings.